Jeffrey Cook

Seeking Structure from Nature

The Organic Architecture of Hungary

With a foreword by
Peter Blundell Jones

Birkhäuser
Basel · Berlin · Boston

Library of Congress Cataloging-in-Publication Data

A CIP catalogue record for this book is available from the Library of
Congress, Washington D.C., USA.

Die Deutsche Bibliothek Cataloging-in-Publication Data

Seeking structure from nature : The Organic Architecture of Hungary /
Jeffrey Cook. - Basel ; Berlin ; Boston : Birkhäuser, 1996
    ISBN 3-7643-5178-0 (Basel ...)
    ISBN 0-8176-5178-0 (Boston)
NE: Cook, Jeffrey; Makovecz, Imre [Ill.]

© 1996 Birkhäuser – Verlag für Architektur, P.O. Box 133, CH-4010 Basel,
Switzerland.
Cover design and layout: Miriam Bussmann, Basel
Printed on acid-free paper produced of chlorine-free pulp. TCF ∞
Printed in Germany
ISBN 3-7643-5178-0
ISBN 0-8176-5178-0

9 8 7 6 5 4 3 2 1

Contents

As a stranger from the New World, I first visited Hungary in 1986 to participate in PLEA 86, the International Passive and Low Energy Conference held in Pécs. In contrast to the predictable architecture of Budapest, I discovered in provincial Pécs new buildings of surprising freshness and originality that simultaneously seemed deeply rooted in place and culture. Here was a unique fusion of a very New World in a special part of the Old World. The architecture revealed a common set of strong values shared among architects who themselves were not always on speaking terms with each other.

Repeated visits throughout Hungary and into Transylvania, to their cities and villages of ancient culture confirmed how this newly created architecture of universal values was also based on the traditional concepts of a particular people, their landscape and their mutual history. A friend and colleague, Victor Olgyay, now on the architecture faculty of the University of Hawaii, accompanied me and added his perceptions on three of these expeditions. Many of his photographs are included in the illustrations.

My support by Arizona State University as Regents' Professor must be recognized. But it was a grant from the Graham Foundation that convinced me of the integrity of the organic architecture of Hungary. I had proposed a study of contemporary organic architecture in the USA and Europe. Yet in Hungary, I found a particular philosophic coherence and a large body of buildings, in contrast with the often isolated and rural organic architecture elsewhere. The social conscience of organic architects in Hungary was also often missing elsewhere.

The friendship and support of many Hungarian architects must also be acknowledged, including some whose work is in other directions. Rather than focus on the personalities of these very distinct architects, I have sought the common thread of design commitment through different building types. As a foreigner without skill in their difficult native language, I have found architecture to be the common language.

The central idea of organic architecture – the alternative tradition of the Modern Movement – is that buildings should be responsive to place and society. Frank Lloyd Wright, its leading North American exponent, spoke of "the thing growing out of the nature of the thing". Hugo Häring, its greatest European theorist, insisted that "we should not express our own individuality, but the individuality of things". Both considered that buildings should be designed in an utterly specific way – specific to purpose, place, culture and climate. The identity of a building was to be deduced from the circumstances that it was destined to serve, the architect being seen as an interpreter of the given situation rather than as straight creator.

The organic approach had a handful of highly distinguished followers such as Alvar Aalto and Hans Scharoun, but it became overshadowed in mid-century by the tendency known as the International Style. This was typified by the universalist work of Ludwig Mies van der Rohe. Left deliberately flexible rather than being made specific to purpose, its buildings were made in essentially the same way whether they were in Reykjavik or Johannesburg. Its uniformity was considered a sign of strength, demonstrating the dominance of a new rational and scientific world order in place of divisive old superstitions. It lent itself to techniques of mass-production that, after the success of Henry Ford, seemed inevitable; and it gloried in the precision of the machine-made detail. It accepted a profligate use of energy both in its production and in its operation. In various guises it spread around the world and, shorn of the subtleties that distinguished the work of its founders, it soon became banal, repetitive and oppressive. A growing population had to be housed, and International Style architecture lent itself to mass-production and prefabrication – usually in reinforced concrete. Rows of endless slab blocks sprang up everywhere in Europe during the 1960s and 70s, but some of the largest were in the East, where ideological programmes were relentless, omnipotent and less subject to criticism.

The recent organic movement in Hungarian architecture, which centres on the figure of Imre Makovecz, was born out of a reaction against this architectural dead-end, and against the kind of centralised bureaucratic control which it represented. This reaction embraces a number of issues. First, it shows the yearning for a specific Hungarian identity as opposed to the technical anonymity which went before. The appointment of Makovecz to design the Hungarian Pavilion at the Seville Expo demonstrates the extent to which the new architecture is now accepted as a national symbol, but in its creation of churches and community centres for small rural communities the movement has been more specifically local. Second, in place of heavy prefabrication the new architecture seeks a revival of craftsmanship using natural materials, particularly indigenous timber. Third, after a period in which form had largely been dictated by production processes, the new movement rediscovered its sculptural and evocative potential, and indulged a fascination with the plant-like and the animal-like. It is this that has made the work popular in the outside world. Fourth, by using local low-energy materials such as timber, it shows some ecological responsibility. Fifth, in building for small communities, the new movement has promoted local participation, which helps bind the buildings to their cultural setting.

In its intense specificity, the new Hungarian architecture could be seen as a return to the Organic Modernist tradition. Its leaders do acknowledge the influence of earlier organicists, particularly Wright, but the work does not show his sophistication, nor that of an Aalto or an Erskine. Its deliberate primitivism suggests rather different priorities. It could be dubbed "Critical Regionalism" in Kenneth Frampton's terms, but some of the weakest work is image-driven enough to be called Post-modern. There is a real danger of it becoming part of a stage-set Hungary geared more to the tourist industry than to the development of an authentic cultural identity, though these two are not now easily distinguishable.

As with many movements, the earliest work was the most powerful, and it remains to be seen whether the sense of purpose and imagination shown by the founders will be retained. Certainly it needs to develop beyond its initial primitivism and to deal with the essential conflict between the primeval forest and the age of the computer. Whatever the judgement of history, Jeffrey Cook has done us the service of a very full first documentation, setting together a body of work which can be critically scrutinised in its delight and its contradictions, its irony and its nostalgia. This will be an important story if what happened in Hungary turns into a model for the rest of Eastern Europe.

To Be Hungarian

A Place for Organic Architecture

Hungarians today call their country "Magyarország" after the Magyars, believed to be the most prominent of the equestrian tribes from the east who settled throughout the whole Carpathian basin in the 9th century. The Hungarian tribes, including the Magyars are unrelated in origins or tongue to any other ethnic group in Central Europe, where they are surrounded by Germanic peoples to the West, and primarily Slavic peoples on other sides.

For a thousand years, Hungaria, the land of the Hungarians, was a polyglot and ethnically mixed territory, occupied by smaller numbers of other peoples. It was a Kingdom with a multi-national state and complicated ethnic origins. Under the last Habsburg emperor before World War I, the large Hungarian banknotes were lettered in eleven languages; Magyar, German, Czech, Slovak, Polish, Romanian, Ruthenian, Slovenian, Croatian, Serbian, and Italian.

But before the First World War in a period of increasing tension and anxiety neither a genuine political democracy nor social equality were in place. The toll of suffering and losses from that war were compounded by the political and social unraveling of the 1918 Revolution. What started as a confrontation of the new industrial working class against the old social order, expanded as armed conflict with neighboring nations, and became a rally of nationalism. When the Peace Treaty for Hungary was finally signed on 4 June 1920, it was not in the splendid Hall of Mirrors of the Palace of Versailles, but in the modest Trianon. Hungary lost two-thirds of her prewar territory and 59 percent of her population to surrounding countries as part of "the Balkan solution".

Today, Hungary, situated in the center of the Carpathian Basin of Central Europe extends over 93,030 square kilometers. With less than one percent of the land area of Europe, it is approximately the size of Portugal or the USA state of Indiana. But with a home population of ten million in 1960 and ten and a half million in 1990, it has a population density larger than France, or Austria, her neighbor to the west.

One cannot be Hungarian without the year 1956 having an extraordinary emotional importance. But it is a topic which even today is rarely discussed. It was an event all wish had never happened, but one that rocked the world and violently shook every Hungarian who lived through it. Already it is a historic date like 1526, 1848, 1867, or 1918, because the younger generation did not experience those tragic "Thirteen Days that Shook the Kremlin". This Hungarian uprising against the Russian occupation and their communist socio-economic system was brutally crushed.

As a modern European country, Hungary emerged late, in spite of the thousand-year-old identity established by István I (Stephen I), who became Saint Stephen. István's father Géza prepared the ground for Hungary's Christianization and had his son baptized. Istaván received his crown from Pope Sylvester II in 1001 and then ruled over a Christian state gradually attaching itself to Western Europe. The design of Stephen's glittering 11th century crown of filigree gold and colored enamel figures may epitomize the dilemma of being Hungarian. The upper part bearing the cross with two vertical golden bands is assumed to be of Western European origin, the lower part with its horizontal hooplike diadem probably came from Byzantine Emperor Michael VII Ducas. No one dares to straighten its famous bent cross that is said to point to the west. But as the most treasured object of Hungary, it is no longer a symbol of monarchy, but of unique sovereignty, an icon of political independence that must not rest on anyone's head. The crown of St Stephen represents a supreme mystical force, the quintessential expression of Hungarian independence.

The joining of East and West anticipates the political and cultural dilemma of the land-locked Magyars for the next thousand years. Dualities have continually threatened the Hungarians. As a Christian monarchy from 1001 on, Hungary often acted as a defensive bastion for Western Europe in the face of eastern invaders.

The infamous battle lost at Mohács in 1526 initiated 150 years of Turkish occupation and a tripartite division of the country. This period of devastation included religious and political persecution. The endless battles explain why so few buildings of that era survived, and why they are so treasured. The peace of Karlovitz of 1699 placed almost all of Hungary under the Habsburg Monarchy. When in 1787 the German language was introduced to replace Latin as the medium of administration and justice it was only one of many measures of reform often instituted by foreigners that added to the resentment of occupation.

During the so-called Reform Age between 1825 and 1848 the folk tongue of the Magyar was transformed into the Hungarian language and a new literature flourished. The failed 1848/49 war of independence with Austria was followed by the stalemate of nationalistic passive resistance. Until the Austro-Hungarian Compromise of 1867 there were many failed attempts at independence. The Compromise, "Ausgleich", effectively created Budapest as a joint capital with Vienna of the Austro-Hungarian Empire. But the Dual Monarchy allowed the internal autonomy of historic Hungaria. Its territory of over 300,000 square kilometers was coincident with the Middle Danube basin between the Carpathian Mountains and with a heterogeneous population in which just over half were Magyars. With prideful showmanship the Hungarians began constructing Budapest as a capital that would outshine Vienna. To direct this explosive growth, an international competition for the city plan was sponsored in 1871, the first such undertaking in Europe. Budapest was also characterized by the urban applications of new technologies: the underground Metro of 1896 before Paris, the electric tramway 1887, the cable car as well as its bridges and early use of cast iron including two Eiffel structures.

The Elizabeth Bridge (1902) long held the world record for a single span chain bridge. The population of Budapest grew from 280,000 in 1869 to 618,000 in 1896, the year the country exuberantly celebrated its millennial anniversary. Among the many spectacular events was a temporary "Open Air Ethnographic Museum" with typical objects of country life and folk art, a collection that became the core of the modern permanent Hungarian Ethnographic Museum.

The emergence of the nation in the latter half of the 19th century coincided with the blossoming of Budapest as a capital and a great city. The enthusiasm for cosmopolitan and international city culture was countered by the ethnic and nationalistic content of the folk culture of the countryside. Thus Art Nouveau often creatively fused with romantic nationalism in the art and architecture. From the late 19th century these competing qualities of uniqueness and worldliness dominated the cultural rhythms of both country and capital as well as the relationship of Budapest, the capital with its present 2 million people, to the countryside and the provincial cities. This cultural dialectic between city and countryside emerged generations later in the evolution of a distinctly Hungarian organic architecture.

The economic and urban explosion of Budapest at the end of the 19th century, fueled by nationalistic ideas of culture and patriotism, coincided with European architectural romantic nationalism. In Hungary historicism, especially neo-classicism, became too closely associated with Western imperialism. Thus explorations of Eastern architecture were considered more sympathetic with the country's ethnic origins. Moorish, Byzantine, Islamic and even Hindu streams were explored. The search for genuine roots resulted in the leading nationalistic examples of architects Lechner and Kós.

The first and the most original of the Hungarian architects during the period that paralleled National Romanticism in Northern Europe was Ödön Lechner (1845–1914), who is still considered a brilliant maverick. His most successful designs were the results of competitions, as all public buildings then were submitted to competition. Lechner's winning designs were built within a very close time period mostly in Budapest. The Museum and School of Applied Arts, Iparmüvészeti Múzeum (1891–96) in partnership with Gyula Partos was quickly followed by his Institute of Geology, Földtani Intézet, (1896–1899), and the former Postal Savings Bank, Postatakarék Pénztár (1899–1902). All were urbane in spite of their stylistic invention. Colorful decorative idiosyncrasies included tattoo and flicker effects as well as embroidery patterns, some derived from peasant costumes. Art Nouveau, Sezession, Jugendstil, and Liberty Style had been eclipsed by the nationalistic and influential goals of Lechner. "Since a Hungarian form language was not existing; we shall make one." he proclaimed. More subtly in June 1906 Art magazine, Müvészet, Lechner wrote:

> The language of form has great power of suggestion.
> Its ability to conquer is stronger than that of the literary
> language. Hungarian language has difficulties in
> spreading among the foreign tongues. People (of foreign
> tongue) do not understand it, nor do they want to –
> for political reasons. Therefore, we have to assist the
> Hungarian tongue with the help of the Hungarian
> form-language which communicates through the eyes.

Aside from a progressive movement known as the Pre-Modern, a third architectural direction of this period was "The New Youth," or "The Young Ones" under the influence of Ede Wigand Thoroczkay. They deliberately wanted a new national style that would synthesize the latest technology with traditional folk architecture. But "The Young Ones" were more conservative than Lechner. Their most talented leader, Károly Kós

(1883–1977) wrote, "The basis for our constructive art is the Middle Ages and the basis for our national art is folk art". On their research trips through the countryside and especially in Transylvania they found the strong architectural qualities that guided their work and avoided the skin deep surface decorations of Lechner. Asymmetrical composition, powerful roofs, plain walls, and picturesque silhouettes informed even their most urban buildings.

Most loved and completely taken for granted are the buildings by Kós in Budapest at the Zoo. The forms and proportions from Transylvanian villages are reinterpreted in designed landscapes that use natural materials in a deliberately tactile way. Kós and his young colleagues were also inspired by the English Pre-Raphaelites and the Arts and Crafts Movement. They embraced the writings of John Ruskin and William Morris, and took the Finnish National Romantic Movement as a model for preserving and renewing the pure forms of language, music and three-dimensional forms. Just as in Finland the Karelia region became the source for a new but truly national architecture, in Hungary the regions of Transylvania and especially Kalotaszeg became the touchstone for "the Young Ones of the Second Generation".

Thus after the First World War, when through the 1920 Trianon Treaty over five million Hungarians became part of Czechoslovakia, Romania and other surrounding countries as part of the Balkanizing of central and eastern Europe, Károly Kós (1883–1977) deliberately returned to reinforce his traditional culture in Transylvania. The last train to leave Budapest for the now separated Transylvania did not have a passenger car, so Kós rode in the engine. At the crest of his architectural career he returned to his 1910 summer home, Crow Castle at Stana, Sztána in Kalotaszeg and an hour by train from Kolosvár. It was not a station stop but the steam engine stopped briefly.

In Transylvania Kós became a cultural patriot. Full of ideas he began with the concept of a tiny republic of 16 villages. It never happened. But his organization of writers, teachers, and experts in agriculture became a vehicle for the evolution of local cultures, and critical to the well-being of countryside. A short quote from Kós was used years later on the opening page of the 1973 manifesto "Only From Pure Sources":

I have learned everywhere that in every great nation
the father's work is continued by his descendants.
We see the same thing, North and South.
But when we come home, everything that is ours is
undervalued.
Because our home is not yet ready, and because
we don't yet have ready culture and ready art, it is
much easier to bring the ready-made from abroad.
First we should make that culture ourselves. We should
with great effort gather the stones scattered from all
over the country, to build in our own image.
For this task one must have both faith and fanaticism,
for it requires a tremendous amount of work.

Within his lifetime Kós became a living legend, not just for the design of his buildings, but for the potent example of his whole life including the model of passive cultural resistance.
Within Hungary, the Trianon Treaty had dismembered the historic heterogenic Hungaria, the lands where the Hungarians live, and left only those parts where Magyars were in the majority. For the first time Hungarian became synonymous with the Magyar. The ethnically simplified country plunged into a financial and psychological depression that lasted into the 1930s when modernization and growth began again. During the 1930s national romanticism faded in architecture. But architects used native examples of the village vernacular to fight the sterility of internationalism. Although the "Village Research Movement" increased visual appreciation of the rural village and folk culture, there was the recognition of the political, economic, and hygienic backwardness of peasant life. Like the musical composers Béla Bartók and Zoltán Kodály, the architects "looked not only for architectural forms, but also for intellectual values and cultural connections to use in their works".
Architecturally the Bauhaus and the new International Style came late to Hungary. Starting in the 1930s, Farkas Molnár is often identified as the first modernist architect in Hungary with his white weightless asymmetrical villas. As a former colleague of Walter Gropius, and as a member of the Hungarian committee of CIAM, he was regarded as a leading figure of the avantgarde. But the Bauhaus approach with its German associations, its cosmopolitanism, socialism, and its importation from the decadent West was never very popular in Hungary. Most of the Bauhaus-inspired buildings were in Budapest, commissioned by a segment of the progressive but politically left upper middle class. Yet from the mid 1930s to the end of the 1940s international modernism became the vocabulary of most architects.
Again with World War II, the political and military mishaps of Hungary were ultimately disastrous and devastating. As elsewhere in Europe, physical destruction and lack of capital added to the political dilemma after the war. By 1951 fear from the oppressive political dictatorship under Rákosi had already quieted debate in all fields including architecture. The direction of Hungarian architecture was dictated in September/October 1951 "Épités-Épitészet", Designer-Architect:

Our cultural future will depend on how our writers and
artists will relate to the socialist culture of the Soviet Union.
How do we want to learn from it?

At the 1952 Congress of Hungarian Architects the intention was to "give up the imperialist, bourgeois architectural theories," with their "cosmopolitan and antihuman" content and to "learn from the exemplary architecture of the Soviet Union". From a practical point of view this ultimately meant a mobilization through the 1960s toward the mass production of worker housing. The heavy-handed Russian prefabrication method of panel construction was mandated. This was in spite of the existence of much more technically refined and architecturally interesting systems invented and demonstrated by Hungarian architects and engineers in the 1940s. As elsewhere, the rebuilding of the country used an anonymous modern industrialized system that quickly brought minimum modern standards of accommodation and amenity. Reaction, at first silent, was immediate and continuous. This soul-less panel construction was not architecture. While being Russian, it clearly was not Hungarian.

Frustration about the rigor of such socialization programs affected all aspects of life. In 1951 the targets of the Hungarian First Five Year Plan were increased by 60 %. But the demands and exploitation of these economic goals were compounded by political totalitarian techniques and the suppression of religious and intellectual freedom. The unrest that exploded as the October 1956 Hungarian Uprising was ruthlessly quenched. "We are cut and fallen like wheat in a reaper" wrote a student vainly pleading for intervention from the West.

After 1956 the country seemed to be a monstrous lie. Yet János Kádár, the Soviet-backed leader of Hungary, very slowly but by absolute necessity hesitantly led the country toward a more open society. Before 1964 the practice was that "anyone who is not for us is against us". Then Kádár changed this to "who is not against us is for us". Quietly Kádár allowed a soft and almost invisible evolution. Some small enterprise was allowed. In the 1960s it was still possible to find handmade shoes and shirts in Budapest. Doctors might have private prac-

tices and small shops might be permitted, which were unknown in adjacent Czechoslovakia and East Germany. The slow Hungarian path toward a liberalization behind the Iron Curtain led them to increasingly ask whether it was on their Eastern or Western frontier.

Ultimately the 1956 Hungarian Uprising anticipated the dramatic collapse of the USSR monolithic grip on half of Europe, and the political transformations of 1989. The last Russian soldier left Hungary on 30 June 1991, the end of a unique era, and already surprisingly remembered with a certain nostalgia. Within that period, the fragile balance under Kádár was painfully consolidated with an unspoken pact: If you forget 1956 and all its aims, in return we will allow you to make a tiny fortune. But as Hungary slowly complied with this compromise as the "most cheerful barracks" of the Eastern Block, other goals than private gain required another strategies. Resistance to the anonymity of the Kádár version of Hungarian life including the preservation of human dignity, and the enhancement of identity also required a creative vision of another kind of Hungary. For a handful of architectural students who were in University during and just after the 1956 Uprising, the ruthlessness and anonymity of the emerging built environment was the challenge.

Thus a new architecture was invented in communist Hungary. It originated during the darkest days of the cultural occupation, during the 1960s and 1970s. Later they called it "organic", inspired by the freedom and sense of belonging of original American architects such as Frank Lloyd Wright and Bruce Goff. By June 30 1991 there were hundreds of built examples of the new organic architecture in Hungary, and many more had been designed such as the memorable and popular Hungarian pavilion at Expo 92 in Seville, Spain.

The Hungarian organic architectural movement was radical because it originated fresh and basic frames of reference that

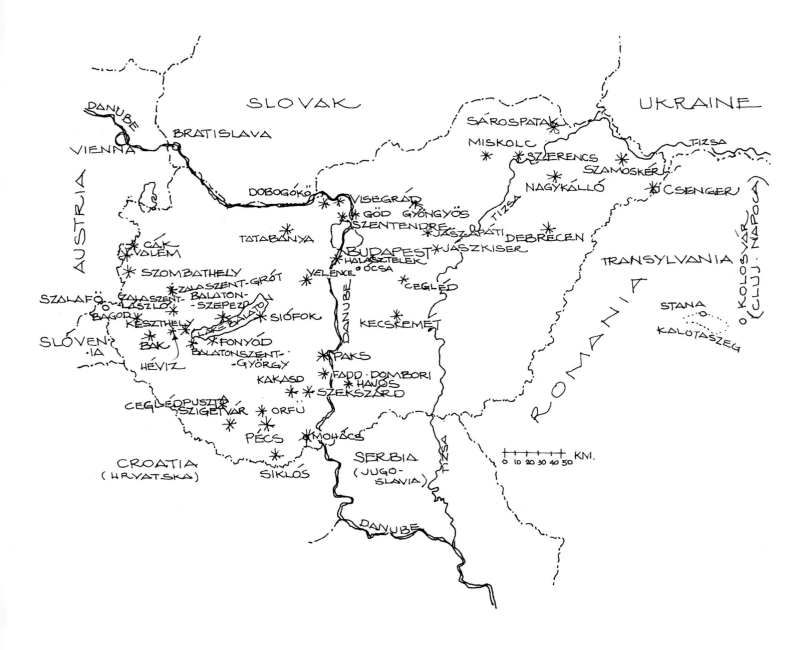

were substantially more critical and fundamental than the continuity or revival of earlier architectural ideas. It attempted to establish deep roots in the particulars of the local physical landscape as well as the cultural landscape. Thus it addressed both the natural and national contexts. Both the prehistoric and the prememory were tapped. Ethnic and national as well as supranational, it sought fundamental ecological and human themes. Thereby universal values were revealed by tapping a local and particular place.

By inventing a new architectural design vision, it was necessary to simultaneously create a new delivery system – a means of offering design service, of insisting on participation by users, and of completing construction within material, budget, and cultural limitations. It meant a new apprenticeship for designers, and creative new architectural forms using the ordinary materials and construction methods that were available and accessible. This comprehensive shared set of beliefs and values meant inventing a new architectural culture.

Only From Pure Sources

György Csete and the Pécs Group

"Only From Pure Sources" was the name of a manifesto exhibition in 1973. Its cover showed a tulip, a Hungarian folk motif, and a geodesic dome, a late 20th century structural concept. This manifesto proved to be the most critical activity of the Young Studio in Pécs, now known as the Pécs Group. Their pivotal public event came as one studio within a large state planning and architectural office, Baranyaterv. It synthesized the confluence of divergent cultural and educational experiences in a city considered provincial, far enough away from Budapest, the capital. This studio of young and like-minded architects that worked and lived together in Pécs, a two thousand-year old city with Roman foundations. In the southwest of Hungary, Pécs and its immediate area are often thought of as the Mediterranean of Hungary since the climate is softer and the lifestyles are more open. The continuous south-facing slope of its large protective limestone valley supports vineyards. The limestone has always been mined, so caves for wine are both natural and man-made. The city has always been a religious and intellectual center; the first university in Hungary was founded there in the 14th century. More recently it has been a center for uranium mining.

Included in the seeds of the Pécs Group were those planted by György Csete. Born in Szentes in 1937, his formative years were during World War II. His father was an army officer assigned to hunt down communist partisans in the mountains. After the war was over, and the communists came to power, the father went to prison and the son was a member of a persecuted family. Although Csete managed through persistance to get into the Technical University of Budapest and earned the architecture degree in 1961, he has never been able to become a professor. Yet he has taught there part-time since 1964. In 1956 during the Hungarian uprising Csete was in his first year at the Technical University of Budapest. Csete can point to the spot along the nearby Petöfi Bridge where he threw his rifle and unspent ammunition into the Danube and went home when the revolution was crushed. He remembers indelibly a Russian statement of those times repeated by a classmate: "Your job is not to think but to learn." Csete has always done both, at great price.

Csete early became interested in the sources of folk culture, and the form of shelter that naturally originates in the gesture of protection using local materials. His university thesis, a proposal for a new Museum at Esztergom, the ancient capital of the Catholic Church, had forced him to consider what might be the specifically Hungarian quality in architectural design. Contributing to this study was the Director of the Museum, László Várgha, a senior professor at the Technical University.

Várgha was an ethnographer with a strong commitment to peasant architecture. His one semester course in folk architecture covered the whole territory of larger Hungaria and all ethnic groups including Germanic, Slovak and Saxon. He himself had documented over 2,000 houses. Part of his comprehensive technique was to return to houses every 10 years to record deaths, births and changes in lifestyle as well as architectural adjustment thus emphasizing the interpretation of all aspects of integrated material culture. As a folk historian at the time of mass production of industrial housing and of minimal concern with craftsmanship and refinement in building, his message was that folk culture was a part of Hungarian history.

Csete entered and won a number of design competitions soon after he graduated. His normal professional assignment was the design of industrial buildings, in Országos Érc-és Ásvány-bányák in Budapest, the design office of National Mines for Metals and Minerals. As a part-time instructor in the Technical University, Csete began to prepare lectures and design studio exercises using a kind of applied ethnology. For instance he restricted design to the use of traditional materials such as wood or adobe, and explored the ordering systems of folk art forms. Included as students in a 1965 class of Csete at the university were Zoltán Bachman, Tibor Jankovics, and István Kistelegdi.

Their design exercises focused on organic directions following geological, plant and folk architectural images.

They continued working together as a small team who shared a common interest, especially on competition entries aimed at finding a new vernacular. The next year, outside of school this group collaborated in a number of design competitions including a summer youth camp for Velence and a scheme for the national theater in Budapest. When Tibor Jankovics and István Kistelegdi graduated in 1968 they were hired to join a new studio deliberately intended to bring young blood and fresh ideas into Barayaterv, the design office for Baranya County in Pécs. Later several of their classmates also joined the so-called "Young Studio". As was typical at that time, fresh graduates went immediately into large state design offices. There were no private architectural practices.

In Pécs this group of recent graduates attempted to continue its special interests. While working as the Young Studio within the large regional professional collective of the Southwest Hungary Design Office, Barayaterv, the need was expressed for a unified approach to design. By 1970 they had convinced their superiors Robert Mischl and István Eördögh to hire György Csete, their former instructor to come to Pécs to head the Young Studio. This act within a large bureaucratic state organization continued a belief in progress and renewal by infusing young and new enthusiasms, in spite of the times when change was unwanted and new ideas were considered dangerous. Indeed, the practice of a more adventurous modern architecture continued in Pécs in the 1970s and early 1980s by the regional state design offices as evidenced in many interesting local buildings.

During vacations and holidays in 1971, Tibor Jankovics and Péter Oltai initiated their own study tours to the remote locations of old Hungarian culture. In the far west of Hungary in the Örség borderland valleys near Austria, they visited the clustered farms of Pityerszer, part of the extended village of Szalafö. Here the agricultural practices of animal husbandry had maintained old farm building traditions such as courtyard planning as well as the "smoky" room – the cooking and living space with built-in stove but no chimney. Lofts of dark wood with thatch roofs cantilevered over whitewashed adobe walls were another typical feature.

Even more inspiring was their study trip to parts of Erdély, or Transylvania, where Jankovics had lived until 1949. Once part of Hungary it was transferred to Romania in 1920 as part of the Balkan resolution following World War I. Since then, some Hungarians have regarded a visit to Transylvania in the same way that classically educated northern students of another era would take the Grand Tour to Italy. It was a kind of finishing school during or at the end of academic studies, perhaps to be

Hungarian House on the Border of Transylvania, mid 19th century. Adobe or mud brick walls, thatch roof, and stork nest. Woodcut by Károly Kós, 1934.

repeated many times through an active life. It was a trip through time and space to the living repository of ancient and honored culture. In Transylvania it is claimed one can find the purest Hungarian language and customs. Through the mountain valleys, settlements have been in the same place since the great Hungarian migrations from central Asia of a thousand years ago. Intermingled are settlements of Romanian Saxon and other Germanic peoples, each several centuries old.

The tradition of living in villages or towns means that the isolated farm house is an exceptional prototype in Hungarian culture. Villages were spaced every five or six kilometers since two to three kilometers was the limit to walk into the fields to work. Especially in the small towns there might be Slavs, Germans, and Magyars, and there would be some mix of religion. Catholics, the varieties of Protestant including the Lutheran and Reform Church, as well as Jews were represented, although individual villages might be relatively homogenous. The tolerance of different belief systems as understood from childhood continues as a memory today by those who were children in Hungary before World War II; an idea that dominated much of the polyglot culture of Hungaria in the Carpathian Basin before the 1920 Balkanization.

In 1972 Jankovics again made a study trip to Transylvania. This time he visited Károly Kós, the brilliant architect who chose to return to Erdély in 1920 when Hungary was partitioned. Their conversations were tape-recorded, and groundwork was laid for yearly meetings. But this had not been the first contact. When fresh out of school in 1968, Jankovics had hitchhiked through Transylvania and deliberately sought out his hero; Kós was 85, Jankovics was 24, but he found they were on common ground. Jankovics asked his advice on what to see in the district. Kós provided maps and letters to local priests. "I have my brave supporters," he said, referring to the aggressive and antagonist political situation in Romania against Hungarians at that time.

Within Hungary the first reassertion of national identity had just begun since the Russians had crushed the 1956 Hungarian insurrection. In December of 1969, the Hungarian Radio started a Saturday noon broadcast of folk music. Called "Our Musical Mother Tongue", a book based on the series was published in 1973, the same year the article "Are We Using Hungarian Vernacular Architecture?" by Gábor Pap was published in the art magazine Müvészet.

The year 1973 was to be pivotal for the Pécs Group as they were now known. They had become identifiable. Their national debut with the help of Eva Molnár, an art historian, was a series of lectures and a graphic exhibition in the "Nest," Fészek, of Budapest, the old actors and artist club from the turn of the century. They were introduced by Károly Kós on tape

Traditional Farm Building, Emeletes Kástu, in Szalafö matches the manifesto description of the three parts of a house: the pliable human zone, the constructive structural spanning zones, and the gigantic roof providing a sculptural conclusion.

Detail of Farm House, in Szalafö, anticipates the modern organic, not just in use of local materials, but in the dominance of the sheltering roof and in the hooded openings.

who was 90 at that time. The lecture presentation was in three parts: "Our Folk Heritage and Architecture", "Only From Pure Sources", and "Our Future in Architecture". The content was summarized in a document titled "Only From Pure Sources" and reproduced in 500 copies. Authorship was equally credited to György Csete, Ildikó Csete, Blazsek Gyöngyvér, László Deák, Tibor Jankovics, István Kistelegdi, and Péter Oltai as a continuum.

The Pécs Group identified two great heroes of Hungarian national culture, the architect Károly Kós (1883–1977) and the composer Béla Bartók (1881–1945). Both emerged at the turn of the century as champions of folk culture and both were associated with Transylvania. Bartók was born at Nagyszentmiklós, now Sinnicolau Mare, Romania. He first became aware of genuine peasant music at the age of 24. From then on his career was a dialogue between careful documentation of folk music, and creative compositions inspired and often informed by these studies. Claimed as one of the world masters of musical composition of his time, he is also honored for collecting much Hungarian, Romanian, and Slovak folk music as well as documenting it.

The Pécs Group was interested in Bartók's reflections on how folk music could be manifest in more elaborate contemporary and concert music in many ways. Their manifesto quoted the third and final verse from Bartók's "Cantata Profana: The Nine Enchanted Stags" finished in 1930. Based on a Romanian pagan legend, it synthesized his love of the people, his nostalgia for village life, and his pantheism:

Once there was a grand old dad.
And he had nine beautiful sons.
He did not teach them any trade,
Only to walk the woods and hunt the beasts.
And they hunted and hunted,
Until they became deer,
There in the forest.
Their antlers would not fit through the door posts.

They could only run through the open valleys.
Their slender bodies could not be clothed.
They could only walk under the leafy branches.
Their feet did not step near the ashes of a hearth,
Only in the soft dry fallen leaves and parched grass.
Their mouths could no longer drink from a glass,
Only from clear running springs.

The last line, which is also translated as "Only from Pure Sources", gave the exhibition and its manifesto its title. The Pécs Group asked, "How could our architectural heritage perish with its massive physical materiality, while our musical heritage thrives?" On the concluding page they proposed:

"In the beginning of this century, the folk art movement was not universally successful. Yet the writings and methods of Károly Kós in 1911 and Béla Bartók in 1931 are still ahead of us and still point out unfinished tasks. It is important that we assimilate every human and cultural value useful to us which is available from humanity.

"At the same time it is important that we get to know the treasure of our folk heritage, that we further develop it and retain it into posterity."

"In folk architecture the human environment, the region, mass, space, and creation are the instinctive and conscious work of centuries leading to general laws and results. The best examples of folk art manifest themselves in works of wise judgment, and in the optimum definition of needs, that inform the entire subject of creation."

"We must continually create harmony between man and nature and its creations; when we get acquainted with the new dimensions of space and time; when we live through ideological and societal changes; and when technology offers infinite choices."

"We search for the answers with our work and with our experiments. Anyone can find answers: Anyone who searches, anyone who works experimentally."

The traditional "balance between nature and man is lost; man has forgotten his organic constructive instinct. We are making repeated efforts to regain that lost harmony."

Within the current cultural dilemma what were the lessons? The manifesto proposed to start with the ground, with the earth:

"The earth: The dirt of the earth grows into buildings. The houses, the haystacks, the hills, the mountains are a uniform and organic formation of nature. Man is at one with nature. The formula of man's house equals gradual rising up out of nature and then returning back to be part of it." (Plate 8)

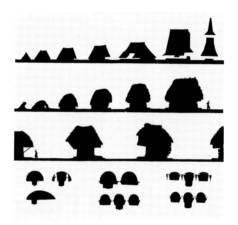

"Only From Pure Sources", Plate 8.

"The house has three components: the earthen body of the building (the pliable human zone); the emphasized cantilevers of the covered structure (the constructional zone); and the peaking roof silhouette (the sculptural conclusion)."

"With its variations of scale, a settlement should not be an obstacle for creating harmony. When a building grows in size, the shape of the roof loses its character, and becomes an alien and anti-human formation. The silhouette, the form of the mass is the decisive factor. It is necessary that a building steps down to human scale in order to create transitions to a pliable and human zone. Thus the formula for a building is the gradual arising form, and returning to the forms of its surrounding. This is a general principle of organic growth. The sculptural possibilities of today's steel-reinforced construction in cities are similar to what mud or adobe did for villages in the past." (Plate 9)

"Only From Pure Sources", Plate 10: Everything you have learned is from nature. Absolute geometry allows intelligence, but it has replaced your natural instincts.

"You have learned everything from nature. But today your absolute intelligence about geometry in space and in time can hardly allow you to touch the petals of a flower. Your deliberate intellectual searchings have replaced your natural instincts." (But nature continues to be the source) in the creation of harmony. (Plate 10)

"The flower is a model of total harmony and integrity created from many organic elements." (Plates 10, 18)

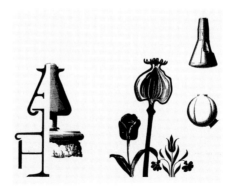

"Only From Pure Sources", Plate 19: Using the nature analogies of the flower and the seed pod, and inspired by cosmic explorations using space capsules, the concept of the Spring House is generated.

"One element emphasized, and with its multiplication and enlargement one can create a series of two level rowhouses so the lines lead back into nature. As the wind blows a waving field of reeds: one element, a single reed forms an infinite system of living, moving variations within wholeness."

"Like a flower, this functioning natural form rises to the light. It is similar to the poppy and its seedpod that grows facing a stone mountain among the big trees. Its materials are wood, formed raw concrete, and rocks, height 16 meters, diameter 8 meters." (Plate 19)

That "functioning natural form" was built as the Spring House at Orfü near Pécs "facing a stone mountain among the big trees". Completed with considerable construction difficulty by 1974 to the 1971 designs of György Csete and Jenö Dulánszky, this symbolic and seminal structure of the Pécs Group made tangible their most inventive effort to develop a native or living architecture. Functionally it had a most ordinary purpose, it was a pump house for the municipal water system.

Deep in the woods, this iconic structure is hidden from view until one walks around a bend, and it is suddenly revealed at the edge of a clearing near a forested cliff. Similar in size and shape to the adjacent trees, the building inspires awe, and a sense of unreality. A patterned poured-in-place concrete ring approximately three meters high forms the base of the building. A short trunk emerges from inside to carry the conical blossoming top. At the very peak is a spherical skylight with crystalline facets. The Pécs Group manifesto of 1973 showed the form of the Spring House as a direct abstraction of a tulip. Beside it was a drawing of a poppy seed pod.

The building is radially symmetrical in plan and has a central spiral stair up inside the structural stem connecting rooms in the two forms. The lower space is for pumps and controls of the water system based on a nearby natural spring. The upper space is an employee retreat, a private space for workers that seems like a place for intense secret rituals. This room at the top of the spiral stair is the only special interior space. But it is so extraordinary, it could be seen as a cosmic chapel. Coarsely crafted of wood it evokes the sense of being inside a flower. The only light enters through a glazed geodesic patterned oculus. Sitting inside the flower, the feeling is only of spirit and sky. On the outside the crudity of the concrete work of the mushroom base makes a rich tactile statement about the rough boards of the formwork, as well as the uneven textures from what some would consider poor concrete work. Here the effect is simultaneously ancient or antique, and emerging or blossoming. The organic growth form of the whole building is reinforced by the revelation of material fibers, crystals, and granules.

The Orfü Spring House seems impenetrable, more of a monument to a new unity of man and nature, than as an enclosure

Spring House, Orfü

Spring House at Orfü, Pécs, 1970–1974 by György Csete and the Pécs Group. Although functionally only a pump house, it became the first major monument of the new organic architecture.

Spring House at Orfü. Both the budding form, and the textures of materials make the design appear as an extension of its setting in nature.

Spring House at Orfü. Looking up toward the zenith through the singular skylight, one seems inside a flower with light focused by a geodesic crystal.

for valves and pumps. It is an amulet of the most fundamental, ecological balance of man in nature. By assuming the form of a shrine and by serving as a shelter for the instruments of water, its water has become sacred. It is truly an architectural "source of life". It celebrates a pure mountain spring, like the last line of Bartók's Cantata Profana.

The 1973 exhibition at Fészek had also stimulated meetings of the Pécs Group with the Master School, Mesteriskola, of the Hungarian Architects Union, and with the Young Folk Artists Studio, Népmüvelesi Intéret, of the Community Education Institute, Magyar Epíteszek Szövetsége. But serious architects did not take them seriously. They were kids from the provinces with curious notions but almost nothing built. Outsiders were amused; but insiders were enthused.

Christmas 1973 was celebrated by members of the Pécs Group visiting Ferenc Kallós, László Debreczeni, and Karoly Kós in Kolozsvár, in Transylvania. To honor Kós being 90, they issued a commemorative poster with his enlarged signature.

But this swell of positive activity reached a turning point in 1975 when the prefabricated housing blocks at Paks with their decorated panels were sufficiently completed to discuss. The old village of Paks, was being dramatically expanded to provide apartments for workers in Hungary's first and only nuclear power plant. The economics of factory-produced, prefabricated concrete panels had to be maintained. This technique of housing construction based on Russian models was already well-developed and used throughout the country by 1970. The Young Studio had been assigned the project. As designers they could not redesign the system, but could only deal with surface treatments and with extensions to the standard panel dimensions. This raised the issue of identity within common objects and mass production which they had already addressed in their manifesto. By looking at the many design variations represented by the backs of wooden chairs, one can see how character and individuality is infused into a standard and even anonymous part of the environment.

"Infinite variations you imagined from a few basic elements. You carved your humanity into wood: Order, beauty and the principles of law; it is the communal law and individual law, general and individual, manyfoldedness and singularity that create harmony in your works. Can this concept perish?" (Plate 14)

"The number of variations is 32,768. It can be evolved by interchanging eight elements. On 5 and 10 story panelized housing blocks you can dissolve the rigidity of boxy elevations, and the sterility of cross wall systems." (Plate 15)

Thus the design logic was introduced to relieve the anonymity of mass produced housing. The mathematics might be challenged since the sum of 32,768 is the result of 2 to the power of 15. Alternatively if one assumes 8 wall different elements

Spring House at Orfü.
Custom detailing of the louvred steel
doors and poured-in-place concrete.

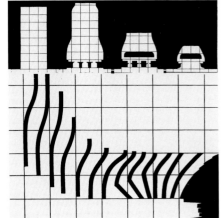

"Only From Pure Sources", Plate 9: How the lessons of transition in small traditional buildings might be applied to larger modern structures.

"Only From Pure Sources", Plate 15: Inspired by the infinite variety of traditional design, three-meter high end panels are proposed to enliven systematized construction of concrete housing blocks.

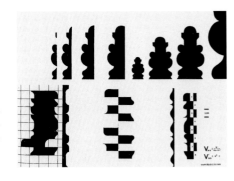

"Only From Pure Sources", Plate 14: Infinite Variations from a few basic elements in the silhouettes of 32 traditional carved chair backs.

"Only From Pure Sources", Plate 6: As the sculptural contours of buildings increase they approach natural forms.

such as the 7 story building as shown, the total of 8 x 7 x 6 x 5 x 4 x 3 x 2 x 1 = 40,320, a larger sum. But the concept was clear.

Under study in 1972, the Precast Panel Apartment Blocks at Paks were not built and publicized until 1975, when they became the trial for this new way of thinking. Countrywide publication of the Paks Apartment Blocks including photographs escalated into a national debate on the relevance of this attempt to humanize the built environment. The public controversy which continued for months primarily in periodicals has been called the "Tulip Wars". The pivotal offensive was written by Professor Maté Major (1904–1986) and published in September on the front page of ÉS, literally "And", the popular name for Élet és Irodalom, Life and Literature.

"By accident I happened to be in Paks and I saw something that was absolutely astonishing. A grey six story box had blossomed with elevations of plant like flat ornamentation painted white from top to bottom. The entrances were emphasized by cup- or shell-shaped elements. Why did it stun me?"

"The young architects of Pécs are innovating. There is no question about it. In the process they have discovered decorative motifs from Hungarian folk art, the handcrafted, and the hand carved wood motifs found in peasant chairs. In other words they conceived the 'tulip' as a metaphor on these surfaces with the intention of becoming a magic implement to regenerate our modern architecture, to make it better, and to make it more national."

"We also had this kind of 'tulip' period in the past. The great Ödön Lechner in the first decades of the Seccession period developed designs using the teacher Joseph Huszka's collections of Hungarian folk ideas together with 'related' motifs from India – hoping to make a national architecture from this curious mixture for the Applied Arts Museum."

"For the Postal Savings Bank, he took Hungarian peasant motifs from the embroidered handkerchief that was part of the coronation regalia of popular Queen Elizabeth (in the apostolic ceremony of Emperor Francis Joseph I in 1867)."

"Between the two World Wars with the evolution of reactionary Hungarian architects this direction ultimately became fascist – proclaiming itself against communism."

Apartment Blocks, Paks

Precast Panel Apartment Blocks at Paks, 1972–1976, by György Csete and the Pécs Group.

Precast Panel Apartment Blocks at Paks. Curved entry walls contrast with the flat walls of the panel construction system.

"László Nagy, with his great reputation as a poet has become a hero and a patron of this movement. He encourages them to follow superficial, external and surface effects, instead of turning them to substance. Because of his patronage and support they now feel free to avoid that difficult discipline. They exercise their firm beliefs by following these cheap solutions. I am convinced that this primitive approach is not the way to rejuvenate our Hungarian national architecture."

Of course it was not by accident that Professor Major happened to be in Paks, and this was not his first article on the subject. Nor was his reference to Lechner's use of an embroidered handkerchief correct. But as a senior academic in Architecture of the Technical University, it became his responsibility to maintain the old order – hence his identification of the folk movement with fascism. The architectural critic Andras Ferkai in 1989 summarized the debate, and explained the events as follows:

"...in the early 1950s the establishment had been transformed. Faithfully following the Stalinist way, industries, the financial institutions and firms, were nationalized. The private practice of architecture ceased. Architects gathered in huge offices established by the state, still did not want to accept the Stalinist style in architecture."

"The political leadership decided to organize a so-called 'discussion', where they could force architects to be obedient. It was very strange that a Marxist professor of architecture, a follower of functionalism, was accused of being the follower of a past style which would not fit with the new social ideas. After this 'discussion', architects were forced to accept the new style."

"The same professor, in the middle of the 1970s, wrote, severely criticizing the organic experiments of the Pécs group; it was a little group of young architects in the southern part of Hungary. They tried to find a new path in architecture; a little bit organic starting from folk or vernacular traditions. This professor, with his criticism, managed to stop the experiment. From this, there developed a heated debate in the pages of different magazines. Eventually sentence was passed on the experiment and the group was dissolved in an administrative way."

The heated exchanges of "tulip" articles were published in a variety of periodicals including Magyar Építőmüvészet, Hungarian Architecture. Especially young architects remember anxiously awaiting the Saturday morning arrival of the weekly Élet és Irodalom, Life and Literature, to follow the next episode. It was perhaps the major public architectural debate in over 30 years. Some consider it the birth of serious architectural criticism in Hungary. Others believe that this incident continues to cripple public architectural debate. Károly Kós supported the young people:

"I don't know what got into Maté Major ... he has an article ... which states: 'Today's architecture is brutal. It is no longer art.

smaller one, Szövterv. As a rebel against the anonymity of international modernism Makovecz initiated his continuous and private search for the basis of a more substantial and authentic architecture. But these early inquiries strongly inspired by Steiner's concept of "embrace and liberate", did not always result in memorable designs. In 1970 his book "Architectural Forms and Movements" was published privately. A diary of intense personal explorations it included photographs and drawings of anthropomorphic forms as generators of space. By using multiple images these graphic descriptions of the shapes produced by movements of the human body also suggested the action of growth, of unfolding wings and harmonic resolution, themes that inspired his creative thinking processes and later became architecturally visible in the forms of his designs. Articles and works, first in Magyar Építömürészet, Hungarian Architecture, between 1966 and 1972, and then in Müvészet, Art, between 1972 and 1975 established his identity nationally in the professional press.

Two structures for Szövosz Camping at Balaton Szepezd in 1966–1967 anticipated future directions. Although defined functionally at the time as a wine bar with restaurant, and a fireplace shelter they are bilaterally symmetrical structures built of substantial, tactile, and identifiable local materials. Battered fieldstone walls are capped by overhanging pyramidal red tile roofs. Both are well-rooted to their wooded hillside overlooking Lake Balaton. But both walls and roofs display those articulations of surface and unfolding of planes that characterize the dynamics of organic architecture as later developed by Makovecz. And like his other restaurant designs of the time, at Valence and Szekszárd, the dominant roof with its deliberate sheltering overhang suggests a deep protective hood sometimes slightly tipped up to allow a discrete view out from within the deep secure shadow.

Between 1971 and 1977 Makovecz worked in Váti, the state planning institute where he was head of a design studio. Again few significant buildings resulted although there were strong shifts in his personal studies, especially toward his examination of folk culture. A significant event was the July 1975 Tokaj workshop. At an artist colony in the wine district of north Hungary 40 teachers, 50 folk artists, and 150 students experimented in applied art and architecture based on folk traditions including the use of native unprocessed materials for construction.

The intensity of this experience and the design potentials of a complete environmental integration had inspired his Duna Restaurant near Szentendre of 1975–1976 and the funeral chapel at Farkasrét Cemetery in Budapest also initiated in 1975 and completed in 1977. In both, the collaborations of interior designer and craftsman Gábor Mezei were critical to the impressive interiors. Most memorable was the mortuary

Duna Restaurant, Szentendre, 1975–1976, by Imre Makovecz with Gábor Mezei.

chapel where a layering of distinct interior profiles were inspired by the repetition of parallel ribs in the roof structures of earlier buildings. This building will be discussed more fully in the chapter on churches and chapels.

The Duna Restaurant, located near Szentendre, in its inner spatiality perhaps represents a turning point. The anonymity of the severe exterior with its clean silver quarter sphere and a lean-to-shed could be dismissed. But the layered rotating spatial definitions of the playful interior are intensely personal. The repetition of wood profiles, the varying definitions of personal space and the integration of electric lights were again derived from the repetitive rib patterns as shown in the exposed structure of earlier restaurants, such as described later on in the chapter on "Roof as Shelter". Here in rotation and alternation they describe a complex three-dimensional humanly scaled interior architecture.

In 1977 Makovecz had an architectural exhibition in Budapest with a handsome illustrated catalogue, his first published monograph. Also in 1977 Makovecz made a critical professional shift. He made a retreat to the woods. He joined the National Forest Organization as their only architect and became attached to the Pilis Forest at Visegrád, 40 kilometers north of Budapest, a hilly preserve overlooking the bend of the Danube. It was a return to basics in the most radical sense. To live in the forest, to choose the materials for construction in their natural state, and to explore their form-giving opportunities in harmony with the human spirit was a profound re-education. He was fundamentally alone professionally, outside the heavy bureaucracy of state architectural offices where he had spent the past 15 years.

During the summer everyone spends as much of the hot season as possible outside Budapest. Those without a tiny cottage or a family house in a village go camping. Already in 1977–1978 Makovecz had completed a series of summer camping structures in the Pilis Forest near Visegrád. As seen in the Picnic Shelters, a rustic architecture was developed through a structural assembly of support ribs and wall planking. Continuous ribs fold wall and roof into a single cup-like hooded form. Each hood is a family food preparation area. The encampment of six hood forms is around a central bonfire – an expression of collective and ceremonial community.

In the sculptural design of Public Lavatories the form goes beyond the provision of lavatory basins and water closets. A single wrapped enclosure is open at the top where projecting ribs terminate against the sky and two totemic columns signify by their carving which is the side for men and for women. The genders are separated by a straight partition that runs the length of the structure but does not confuse the larger statement of enclosure and human wholeness shared by the large open

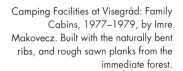

Camping Facilities, Visegrád

Camping Facilities at Visegrád: Family Cabins, 1977–1979, by Imre Makovecz. Built with the naturally bent ribs, and rough sawn planks from the immediate forest.

Camping Facilities at Visegrád: Picnic Shelters, 1976–1977, by Imre Makovecz. Hooded food preparation shelters encircle the central outdoor fire.

Camping Facilities at Visegrád: Toilets and Lavatories, 1977–1979, by Imre Makovecz. Both men's and women's facilities are within the same curved wall enclosure open to the sky.

Camping Facilities at Visegrád: Toilets and Lavatories.

eye to the sky. The plan is the profile of a tulip. Again naturally curved wood ribs bend wall and ceiling into continuously warped surfaces of plank.

Even more adventurous were the cabins, cottages, and workshops. Bent ribs hand cut and trimmed from the immediate forest are organized in rambling plans of almost tunnel-like enclosure with open hooded ends. Sawn boards and shingles overlay the planking as a rough fur providing a textured weathering skin.

This neo-primitive architectural vocabulary climaxed in the 1980 ski resort at Dobogókö, also in the Pilis National Forest in the mountains about 40 kilometers northwest of Budapest. A ski bar and a ski lift, the latest industrialized technology of recreation are completely absorbed by animated rusticity.

Ski Lift and Bar, Dobogókö

The entrance along the west side guides one to enter by sliding along under the protective skin. The south-facing bar with its big windows capped by a tall furrowed brow and horned chimney provides a face. Inside the ski bar neither the central fireplace nor the bar are quite parallel with other parts of the building. With its high dark loft, this is the ultimate of cozy and expansive après ski settings. The friendly power of the natural architectural language of this ski lodge has made it the genesis of further designs that seek to explore building as body, protected by architectural fur.

Particularly in this design Makovecz acknowledges the influence of Herb Greene's "Prairie Chicken" House at Norman, Oklahoma, USA completed in 1961. Makovecz saw beyond its animal-like form and creative use of natural materials to its primordial images and associations such as the great hooded eye that overlooked the prairie protected by lowered horns. Makovecz associates these revelations with his discoveries of the organic American architecture of Frank Lloyd Wright and Bruce Goff while he was still at the University. Greene has stated that "the creature-like metaphors ... cannot be easily verbalized, but they include impressions of a large object, thing or

Ski Lift and Bar at Dobogókö, 1980, by Imre Makovecz. The exterior after a snowfall.

Ski Bar at Dobogókö. View of the interior.

Ski Bar at Dobogókö. Southern facade.

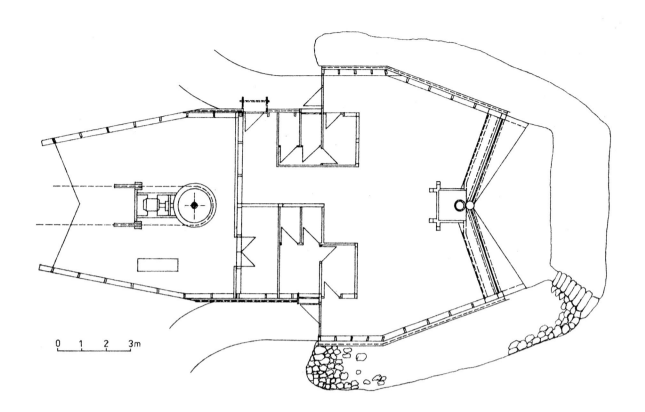

Ski Lift and Bar at Dobogókö. Plan. The ski lift is in one end, and the bar is at the other.

creature, rather at home on or accommodating itself to an expanse of natural prairie".

Makovecz's shaggy coated entity emerges out of the mountain top forest, its formidable rustic shape not formless, its hairy texture of boards not casual. In spite of its great presence, it is approachable and friendly, merging in and out of the natural environment according to season. Against the winter snow, it is the largest object around. In summer and flecked with moss, it all but disappears in the rustling forest. The architect recalls, "... in the November fog ... I suddenly spot the plank-feathered back of the ski lodge at Dobogókö and realize it's there, yes, the reincarnation of the ancient words of architecture".

At the same time in 1980 the Resort Restaurant Mogyoróhegy, Hazel Nut Hill, was designed beside the main access road into the Pilis Park at Visegrád and completed in 1983. It hunches low and close to the ground. There is a certain inevitability about the siting of this fortified, blank walled encampment. At the edge of a sloped meadow, open to the north winds and the view of the Danube with its generous valley, the distant hills of Börzsöny are behind to the north. Blackened horizontal planks are the only visible exterior material. They form the continuous blank fence, the great curved wind shelters as

Resort Restaurant, Visegrád

Resort Restaurant at Visegrád, 1981–1983, by Imre Makovecz. Long horizontal planks supported on the inside by naturally bent timbers structure the sheltered outdoor space and the enclosure of the building.

Resort Restaurant at Visegrád. Blank black planks provide a continous wind break to the north.

well as the restaurant itself, which rises within as a windowless hulk. Wall and roof are a continuum of form. Within the enclosure, windows break through the corners of the restaurant to overlook the surrounding outdoor terrace where tables and benches are built in as part of the wind shelter structures. Similarly the corners of the wind screens are left open to selectively view the sweep of nature outside.

The restaurant itself is strongly protective with its curved plane wrapping of black boards. Its enclosure is also hospitable and welcoming because of the use of natural light. On the interior, the structure is revealed. There is no mystery to the rhythm of Gothic arch shaped timbers that establish the profile of the space. This simple construction method of structural bents and a single layer of plank is economical and generic. It is also understandable to all users. But it is a technique that requires tight fitting of the planks which must be straight and sound. There is no insulation and no place for wires or pipes or ductwork in this basic technique where the architecture is synonymous with exposed construction using local materials.

Much simpler in plan but more complex in materials and detail is the nearby Erdei Müvelödés Háaz, Nature Study and Cultural Center, designed in 1982. When it was completed and dedicated in 1988 Makovecz considered it to be the most important building of his career of more than 30 years as an architect. Sited at the far edge of a flat meadow, it establishes an evocative point of reference for the camp facilities clustered back in the trees next to the rising forest. An earth-covered hemispherical building sited at grade, the structure appears to be a deliberate tumulus, an artificial hillock or mound as once were raised over graves in prehistoric times. This imagery is reinforced by the use of vertical logs as an earth-holding palisade around the main entrance, and the carved eagle heads at the top of the extended gate posts that hold the great wooden doors with their wing-like boarding. Here Makovecz has deliberately built according to the ancient words for these architectural parts: doors are "wings", gateposts are "eagles". The richly variegated slate roofing at the top of the dome appears to have great age. At the summit is a crown-like cresting with tiny gold globes springing out of vertical leaves that conceal an oculus skylight. The grass sod covering the lower roof ties the building back to the earth and provides thermal and acoustic sheltering. The excavated earth has been filled back around the building so it looks like it grew out of the ground.

The building is formed by the interconnection of two concentric hemispheres. Around the perimeter is a continuous series of smaller spaces used as offices, classrooms and other services to support the primary educational activity of the central hall. Inside the centralized hall, the herringbone pattern of boarding between the ribs reinforces the regularity of the skylit space. Natural light also enters through the glazing of the broad entry gates oriented exactly east-west and through small arched windows tunneled through the earth berm. Tree trunk columns are capped with circular zodiac shields painted to honor fishes and animals found in the park. Electric lamps clustered at the top of each column add to the rhythm of the enclosure. On Hungarian Television in 1988 Makovecz described it:

"The building is like a hill. The grass-covered cupola is apparently emerging from underneath the earth, tearing it apart. There is a crown on top. Twelve columns hold the double blue cupola inside. One of the two main entrances is oriented on 21st March to the sun rising, and the other one to the setting sun. Sunshine can come through the crown and its skylight, so

Nature Study Center, Visegrád

Nature Study Center at Visegrád, 1982–1988 by Imre Makovecz

Nature Study Center at Visegrád. Entrance.

Nature Study Center at Visegrád. Great doors shaped like wings and guarded by eagle gate posts provide access to the earth-embraced interior.

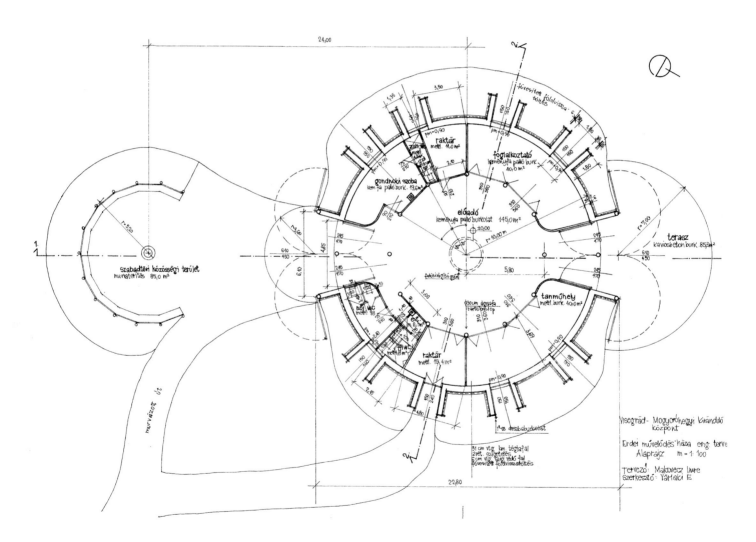

Nature Study Center at Visegrád. Plan, showing central hemispherical hall with two sets of great hinged doors on opposite sides. The surrounding ring of support spaces have small windows that tunnel through the earth berm.

the hall works as a sundial. The sun gave the position of this building in this landscape, and thus the passages of time are marked by design."

Here nature study in a state park of 32,000 hectares is grounded in a womb-like hall and is projected with suggestive illusion to the cultures of other times. All true cultures must ultimately be rooted by understanding nature as embedded in the local soil. The nobility of this earthy architecture speaks of universal harmonies based on intimate knowledge of nature, not stylistic images of national or ethnic identity. Makovecz has created an architecture of participation, not observation.

The gradual depth of primal experience and maturity that Makovecz gained in the Pilis Forest was shared in many ways. Makovecz initiated the first annual summer design and build workshop in the Pilis Forest in 1981. Thereafter they have been organized by architecture students for themselves autonomously, without connection to any organization or institution. It was a time of stifling political repression. So these camps provided a unique circumstance where it was possible to make something from the heart. Being self-organized, students could program each day, selectively inviting resource people such as Makovecz.

The location of the camps was the work space of an abandoned mine, St. Stephen near Visegrád. On a small plateau surrounded by mountainous slopes and overlooking the Danube, it was at once isolated and connected to nature. These camps of two to three weeks focused on the creation and construction of a single project based on local natural materials. Each design was conceived and realized as a cooperative enterprise, just as real buildings can only be achieved by a team effort. The real effectiveness of the camp came from students who repeated the experience for several summers. Thus, organic continuity was achieved interweaving new and old participants with the resource of a place and an idea.

The names of the annual design projects reveal the seminal nature of each year's focus: the Hive 1981, the Cave 1982–83, the Bridge 1982–83, the Road 1984, the Tower 1985, the Sign 1986, the Dancing Barn 1987, the Pod 1988, the Theatre 1989, and the Stone Circle 1990.

The peak attendance was in 1987 with 100 participants. The emphasis was on the development of the internal human being. There was no leader. Makovecz recalled that,

"The therapy of living and working together for a common goal is very unlike the school environment, where the students seem to be isolated. There students are lonely, small individuals in a crowd, without orientation, where people seldom congregate around ideas or pursue and accomplish a purpose jointly. Our summer workshop camps develop skills and capabilities through participation, which the school environment does not provide ..."

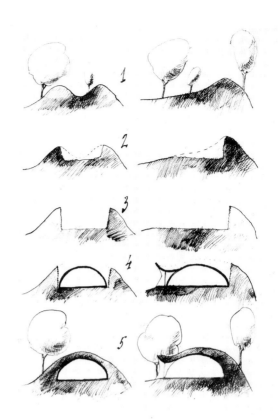

Summer Design and Build Workshop at Visegrád, 1982–1983. The Cave by Ferenc Salamin, sketch studies.

Summer Design and Build Workshop at Visegrád, 1985. The Tower by Gábor Urr, conceptual sketch of proposed structure and finished project.

Bükk Forest National Park Entrance at Miskolc, 1984, by Benö Taba of Miskolcterv. By projecting and twisting the roof structure skyward, a distinctive silhouette is generated in the center of a flat meadow to mark the park entrance.

"Twenty is the age for facing reality. A time for discovering the thoughts of others and understanding the point of their work to be able to create something together. Natural instinctive childhood knowledge together with discoveries made through education can provide the inner power which is the basis of creative pursuit. This personal power makes it possible to get to know oneself and to create a new reality. Strengthened in spirit we can then help others to find their own inner selves. Realization of the existence of this inner power is a laborious process, but failure to search for it is sin against life."

A description of the Pod workshop, written collectively by several of the 1988 participants, summarizes the conceptual structure of these intense summer experiences:

"At the very beginning in spring, everything seemed so simple. We create something, draft it up, and build it in the Summer. But we gradually realized that we all had become characters of a fantastic, almost legendary story which began at the moment when we came together for the first discussion. Such a story only reveals itself to the people who take part in the creation and experienced it. Thus a strange construction appeared before us, not something to be looked at or heard, but simply experienced."

"We experienced an inconceivable thing – the realization of an idea. Such a deeply rooted idea only revealed itself as we approached the conclusion. Only by the time when we, the

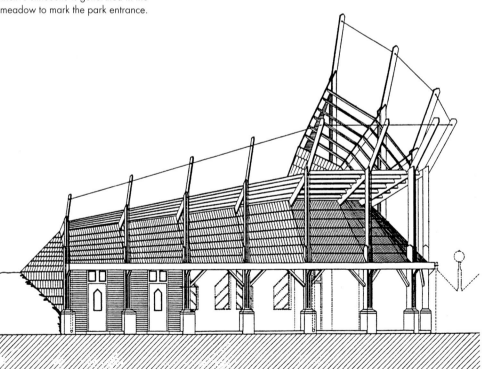

Bükk Forest National Park Entrance at Miskolc. Elevation drawing shows how roof framing is developed from the sweep of lineal pieces.

creators had parted from it, did it become worthy enough to bear its name. The Pod is the symbol of the experience of this creation. This was the experience we left behind as an inheritance in the mine shaft work yard."

The 1984 entrance to another National Forest Park became the subject of a celebratory design in wood by another young architect. Benö Taba designed an Entrance Gate and a Lookout Tower for the Bükk or Beech Forest while working in the state planning office, Miskolcterv. This reception center sits in the middle of a flat grassy meadow against the mountains, at the southwestern corner of the industrial city of Miskolc, along the road that then winds up through the mountains to Eger. The modest requirements for enclosed spaces have been extended and exaggerated as the base for large warped and shingled asymmetrical roofs that screen the view of the immediate mountains and focus on the gateway. Their sloped wood roof planes slice a space in the sky that is magnified by the extension of columns and rafters as carved wooded sabers etched in the air. Notched decorations suggest the imagery of ancient wooden grave markers. Foundations of local fieldstone and exaggerated areas of dark roof deck anchor the combined structures to the ground and to the natural environment.

On axis but some distance away is a second building, an exhibition structure combined with an observation tower that serves as a pivotal landmark. It terminates the end of this meadow with its outdoor exhibits that function as a nature interpretive center. Stone walls and broad stone steps frame the opening in a large wooden domed structure. It is pierced by a tower with its interior stair up the stem to observation deck and lookout, sheltered by a small wooden domed parasol. A fresh decorative design, it imitates nothing in its creative forms. The whole construction took over two years and involved voluntary help as well as skilled builders such as stone masons.

Further east and south in Hungary, the skillfully executed park structures built at the Téka camp outside Nagykálló at the village of Harangod are both playful and suggestive. Indeed some Hungarian architects cannot believe they were permitted to be built in Hungary. Designed and constructed primarily between 1986 and 1989, Dezsö Ekler of Makona, the co-operative practice around Makovecz, is credited as the prime designer. He also represents the transfer of design responsibility from Makovecz to the new generation, who gradually became part of the studios associated with Makovecz. Many of them had taken the summer design camps at Visegrád.

The several Nagykálló structures for summer folk dance and folk music camps beside a lake are particularly interesting in their process of realization. Designs were conceived and built essentially without drawings. Each was put up in a single summer.

Bükk Forest National Park Entrance at Miskolc.

Recreation Facilities, Nagykálló

Dance Barn, Téka Camp at Harangod, Nagykálló, 1986, by Dezsö Ekler of Makona.

Dance Barn, Nagykálló. Through their layout, one-at-a-time during construction, ordinary pine boards become attractive features.

The Dance Barn of 1986 was first. It was erected without elevations and without structural calculations. These were provided afterwards to confirm building permission. The circular plan has a star-like structural pattern that triangulates the light wood framing into a dome-like structure. It is a kind of hat with continuous waves of short overlapped roof boarding that achieve sculpted surface effects. Raised wings or ears provide ventilation at the peak, but are memorable in how they transform the image to multiple identities. Whether as Brunhilda's helmet, or as some distorted hen, the Dance Barn at night is a magical animated place.

Dance Barn, Nagykálló. The sculpted weather skin gives no hint of the regularity of the structural frame behind.

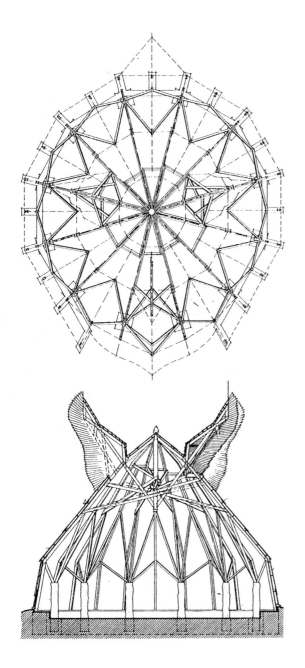

Dance Barn, Nagykálló. Initial sketch from the architect's notebook shows concept based on a tactile skin and dramatic silhouette.

Dance Barn, Nagykálló. Structural plan and elevation reveal the lineal triangulation of roof framing.

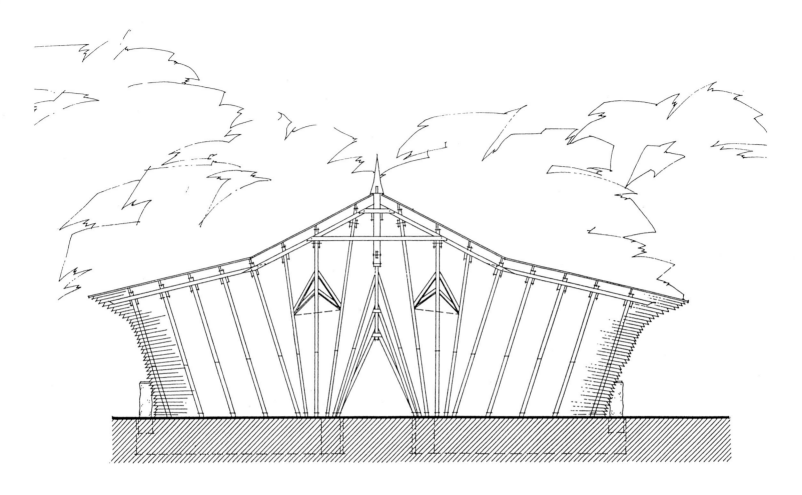

Dining Shelter, Téka Camp at Harangod, Nagykálló, 1987, by Dezsö Ekler of Makona.
Elevation of the bird face whose elementary skin of boarding changes directions slightly where
the line of the roof lifts. The open eyes provide additional ventilation.

Dining Shelter, Nagykálló. An abstract
animated face is generated by straight
lines in both frames and thin regular
lapped boarding.

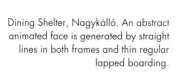

The symmetrical Dining Shelter of 1987 with its horizontal lapped boarding has a simpler image and a lower profile. Again the bird face is there, achieved with the simplest of frame and plank construction. As an articulated tunnel space with a cross axis at midpoint, it is approachable from four directions.

Also symmetrical is the plan and structure of the 1987 Bath building which contains toilets, showers, and lavatories, men on one side, women on the other. Like the other singular structures at the Téka summer camp it is economically fabricated of natural, local materials that make this bold work of elementary architectural enclosure merge with the setting. Its strong, abstract form seems to slide through the hardwoods.

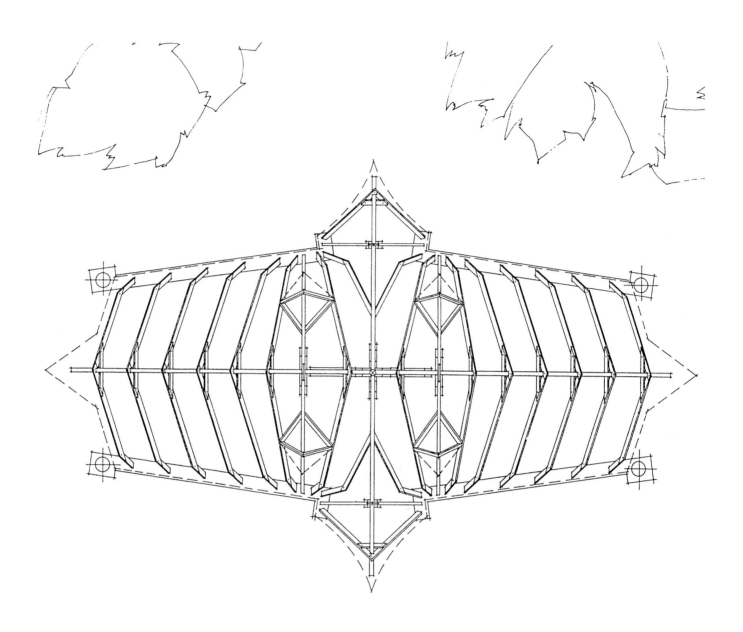

Dining Shelter, Nagykálló. Structural plan shows both simplicity and subtle inflections; only three of the roof frames are vertical.

Baths, Téka Camp at Marangod, Nagykálló, 1987 by Dezsö Ekler of Makona. Lapped board
roof planes float over fieldstone walls, anchored by the central fieldstone chimney.

Baths, Nagykálló. Entrance.

Baths, Nagykálló. The bath roof is open
to the sky, providing a sharp contrast of the
two primary materials.

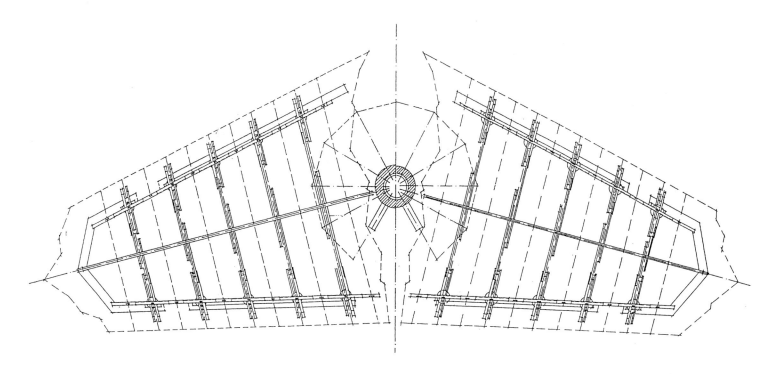

Baths, Nagykálló. Plan. The symmetrical wing shape provides mens' and womens' toilets and lavatories on either side of a central cylinder that contains the baths.

The Reception Hall of 1989 is symmetrical in plan and three dimensions. The building is lodged firmly into the ground but unfolds its wings at the edges as it rises. Its size and scale is uncertain, so it is surprising that it is a small two-story building. The roof boarding is developed as layers of long feathers that allow windows between the ranks. The strata of boards resemble a traditional thatch detail where bundles of reeds are used to reinforce the corners of the roofing.

The Lookout Tower of 1988 sits on top of an exposed natural round hillock and provides a panoramic view of the lake and low-lying countryside. Constructionally, it is the most intriguing building at Nagykálló. Built largely with unmilled timbers, its structure and all its complex joints were designed in the field, and drawn after the fact – just the reverse of a conventional building. Its structural details of traditional jointry are similar to those visible in centuries-old timber belltowers beloved of ancient Hungarian villages. But its helical design introduces a new dimensionality. The double stairs spiral around each other, and the outwardly leaning log columns are impressive for their

Reception Hall, Téka Camp at Harangod, Nagykálló, 1989 by Dezsö Ekler of Makona.
Flurries of featherlike boards are layered or raised to allow windows. The Lookout Tower,
1988, in the background, continues the theme.

Reception Hall, Nagykálló.

non-orthographic command of space. The solid nature of the construction with its structural connections, has the robustness and substance of a newfound belltower.

Each of these free structures is an essay of economy and imagination. Seen as isolated objects or without the population of summer campers they may seem eccentric and unrelated to either daily life or the profound personal revelation. But when experienced as the focal nodes of a village of tents and a community of active outdoor recreation, their life-enhancing, inspiring presence is much more believable.

48

Reception Hall, Nagykálló. Conceptual sketch.

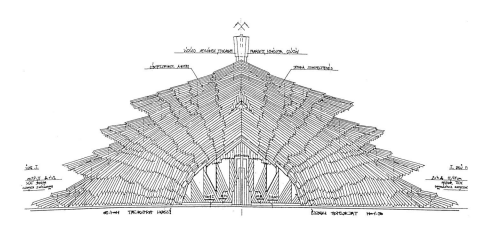

Reception Hall, Nagykálló. Elevation.

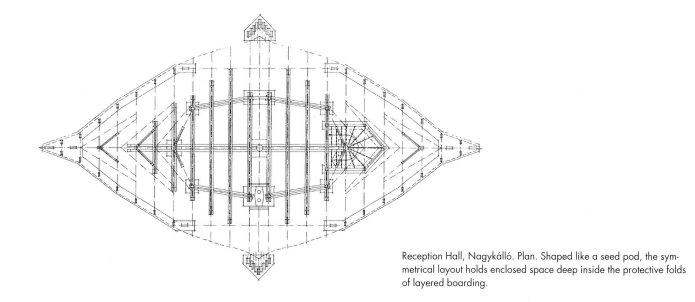

Reception Hall, Nagykálló. Plan. Shaped like a seed pod, the symmetrical layout holds enclosed space deep inside the protective folds of layered boarding.

Lookout Tower, Téka Camp at Harangod, Nagykálló, 1988, by Dezsö Ekler of Makona. The low pastoral landscape of northeastern Hungary with lake, meadows and hardwood forest provide the setting for this summer camp and its structures.

Lookout Tower, Nagykálló. Peeled log columns and milled horizontal timbers interlock, held in place by a variety of structural connections.

In 1983 at the International Workshop Seminar for Students of Architecture, Ráckeve, organized by the Technical University and the Hungarian Section of the International Union of Architects together with the World Federation of Hungarians, Makovecz reflected on the direction of architecture in Hungary and the role of the Visegrád Camp structures:

"Architecture, that secret science of holy orders has come to grief in Europe too. Since the first World War, it is more fashionable to speak about structure, function and perhaps fashion. György Lukács has been proved to be right that architecture is nothing else but practicality and taste. It does not belong to the forms of artistic cognition."

"But it seems that the resigned, forced pragmatism of the past 60 to 70 years has come to an end. Manipulation disguised in the name of beautified and censored human dignity has reached a stage in which it is increasingly clear that it had betrayed itself."

Makovecz admits he is not a follower of Kant. He cannot explain the world in purely rational terms, nor can he separate the subjective from the objective. For him the world could not exist without human presence. So "art or architecture is not a question of form, but of magic", and all his forms intend to have a conscience.

"I have observed I am very primitive", Makovecz notes. But as an outspoken architect, Makovecz became increasingly known in the 1980s not just for his professional engagements getting his unique designs built, but in public forums on radio and television as a national and often controversial personality who advocated for the spirit.

The first occasion when Imre Makovecz was invited by his alma mater, the Technical University at Budapest, to give a lecture was 1990. The world of Hungary, as well as Hungarian architecture, had changed. Makovecz, in his search for meaningful structure, had been an instrument of that change. Still in 1991 the half million book library of the Technical University included two catalogue publications on Makovecz, one report on urban renewal for Pécs by Kistelegdi and nothing else by or about any other of the organic architects, in spite of growing recognition and publications from abroad.

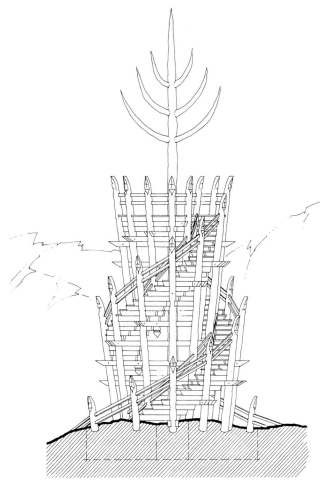

Lookout Tower, Nagykálló. Elevation made after construction shows stairs ascending almost nine meters. Outward leaning log columns add to structural stability and allow stairs to overlap each other. Top of the center-pole spike is over 20 meters high.

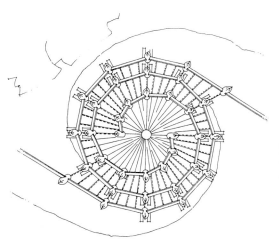

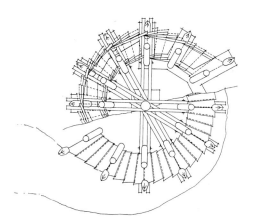

Lookout Tower, Nagykálló. Plans of lookout platform and ground floor, showing pattern of two spiral stairs.

Community and Village Centers

Makovecz and Makona

The traditions of the Hungarian village were totally transformed after World War II. In particular between 1947–1949 new socialist theories were initiated. Imre Makovecz tells the story of the changes in his village of 2,000 in Zala County as he was growing up. There were four food shops, six taverns or small restaurants, and a small factory for spirits. In addition, each circle of special interests had an organization, and a meeting room. The tradesmen, the farmers, the businessmen, the Catholic boys, the Catholic girls, and many others each had their own identification, activities and a place to meet.

With socialist reform all these separate locations were abolished and only one place was assigned for meetings. It was called the House of Culture. The little libraries and many of the treasured records of each organization were consolidated and gradually lost or destroyed. All the shops were closed, to be replaced by one, a "mixed" shop or general store. The six taverns were closed, and a new single one was opened in the old town hall. The spirit factory was shut down, and the equipment was sent to the Soviet Union. Makovecz wrote in Magyar Építömüvészet, Hungarian Architecture, in 1988:

"What was the essence of 'Culture' in the Rákosi-Stalin era? First of all it was destruction. Its main point was destruction itself, the closing of the community houses, the liquidation of the religious institutions, the public humiliation of their former directors and so, the humiliation of the whole community."

"How was this expressed in architecture? ... Buildings had to be altered so that the signs of the former prosperity couldn't be detected ... They hated and regarded as alien everything European that had created beauty and value."

"We got a building with the words of 'House of Culture' written on it and from that time culture meant applause, measured applause. We were forced to applaud our humiliations, our impoverishment, the clean-swept lofts, the destruction of our livestock, and the incomprehensible speeches of merciless foreign leaders who spoke of justice, development, results, and the standard of living, of future and everything else."

"These Houses of Culture got dirty soon, no one maintained them. Outside, the old wooden fences collapsed and the practice of felling the trees and shrubs spread, for they were 'in the way' or they 'kept away the sunshine'. The rows of trees in the streets fell victim to electrification and after the old radios were handed in, the lights lit up in the peasant homes and the 'people's radio' started to speak in which only the Kossuth and the Petöfi stations could be picked up."

The traditional agricultural pattern had been small fields and little parcels owned by small-scale farmers. In addition, there were common open fields and common forests. The herdsmen and shepherds were employed and paid for their work by the village, sometimes in kind. With ultimate socialization everything was taken away, all the animals, all the equipment and all the traditional rights to be replaced by a collective farm with workers paid wages and only one employer. Not a horse wagon was left. This process continued until 1957, one year after the revolt. So each village became one working place where everyone was employed in one business by a single employer.

In 1975 the party decided to create even larger working places. So daily, villagers had to go to work in larger centers and then to travel back to their houses in the villages at night. Since the center for work should also be the center for all other functions, these were removed from the villages. Thus, a village now would not have a doctor or a school, and also nothing was allowed for independent social life whether for workers, teenagers or for old age pensioners.

After the 1956 revolution, population growth severely declined, so the inhabitants of the villages became older, with less and less opportunity for personal or social focus. Without the possibility to work, older people had little interaction in their lives. In addition, those widows or mothers who had only looked after children or elders and did not have the option of working at a state job for 10 years, had no income when they became older. What do such people need? In addition to food, they must have a place to go, to linger, to talk, to play cards. But now there was no school, no library, no place to watch films, or just to meet!

"The accumulated fear, apathy, neglect, and resignation, all the impoverishment and lack of spirit I have seen, have induced a desperate urge of action, understanding, and compassion in me …"

"At the middle and the end of the 1970s the establishment of the large work districts set our work back, and the country as well. We had to reconsider everything. More than fifteen hundred villages were left to themselves without a cooperative, a school, a parson or priest, or a doctor. … We began to con-·centrate on the villages that had lost their independence, to save what could still be saved. We tried to save the village halls decayed in morale, that were physically disintegrating as well."

Makovecz and other architects became activists in partisan reactions against the policies of the Party by participating in changing local life in the villages. Makovecz and his cooperative studios of Makona designed a total of 25 new community centers in collaboration with local unofficial groups outside the system. Seven of them were finished by 1990 when the big political change occurred. These community centers were very different from those social and athletic facilities by the same name in other countries, because in Hungary their origin was a reversal of official public policy. Thus the end of an era was initiated at the grass roots. The goal was a return of old citizen rights and old social patterns. Traveling to the villages in tiny old cars or unheated busses, architects contributed to this creative and healing political process. Makovecz continued his account:

"At the end of the 1970s something had already started that couldn't be stopped. I took up designing village meeting houses one after the other, new buildings, alterations, annexes. We tried to find building materials for these projects almost without financial support."

"I returned for good to wood. I walked in the forest with my clients to find the suitable logs. The consciousness of public interest had to be revived and reconciled among the principals of the cooperative, the council, the county authorities and the population itself. Construction began in an era when the councils had no experience in self-reliant economy. It was the era when increasing individual wealth was radically and dictatorially regulated and when superficial community and national consciousness were encouraged until this would also be plunged into crisis by pauperism."

"Our first village meeting houses were built during the decay of community life and the slow depopulation of the villages. … We solved all the difficulties without the 'help' of writing letters, without threats and without the usual frightened officials. Waiting for our aim, the finishing of the building was different. How many times did we have to travel with Varga to get this or that? I remember the disputes, the worries, the quarrels and the reconciliations, the tight-rope walking between the authorities and the slowly awakening communities."

The village center at Zalaszentlászló, literally "Saint Laszlo in Zala County", completed in 1984, was prototypical. It produced a major architectural statement. But the participatory process was much more critical. The state contributed no money and tried everything to stop it. Permission to build anything took a full year. So village leaders had to work physically as well as vocally and against the wishes of the local officials in re-establishing the rights of the dispossessed. In the end it was not the invention of a distinctive architectural column that counted, but the community accomplishment when the building was dedicated and when "everyone sang the national anthem from their true hearts". Then everyone including the architect knew why he was there and what are the necessary conditions for making a memorable building. But every village has a unique story, every individual his own place related to the official policy of dispossessing villagers from their village.

At Zalaszentlászló, an old house converted into community meeting rooms was too small. It had been the home of a Jewish family who had been hauled away during World War II never to return. Nearby were some ugly small modern shops and restaurant with flat roofs from the 1960s, set back from the single street of the lineal village. These two elements were linked with an L-shaped porch and a large hall by Makovecz. All were embraced under a great common roof in the self-build design.

With a minimal building budget the villagers themselves went to the common forest of the village's agricultural co-op. With Makovecz personally involved in each decision, they roamed the woods to find suitable tall trees to support the great roof. Trees were cut and dragged as trimmed trunks to the site. There they became columns, with branches still attached, transformed trees for the spirits dead and alive of the village. Said Makovecz, "I tried to return the long lost forest to the village". Makovecz first used a tree rather than a column in his 1975 bird watching tower at Lakitelek on the Tisza River where a single live tree was the central support. Makovecz reported: "From the trees of our partly depleted, trackless forests we have built a many-branched, new center, a home for the community. We did not take our occasionally emergent memories of the 'beautiful old Hungarian village' as our model; but rather, the healing, reappearing woods. So that we may find ourselves a home, we preserve the house of the annihilated Jew, and the corrupting planar modern building as well; under the protection of the new roof."

The result was an open courtyard facing the road with living green trees in dialogue with the dead tree columns. A continuous porch allowed entrance to the main facilities from the side, in the traditional Hungarian manner. Since the scale and proportions of village houses were continued, the center became an inevitable part of the streetscape. The approximate ratio of one to one, with plain and white-washed walls equal to strong simple roof forms, was repeated with these stucco walls and its purplish-grey tiled sheltering roof. Because of the pitch of the roof, the sheltering low entrance porch roof rises overhead to 10 meters inside.

The interior is a vast barn-like hall, with a large dance or meeting floor surrounded by seating and a cafe bar. It is a spacious but dark and moody retreat articulated by the placement of tree columns. Separate rooms provide for club meetings and private

Village Center, Zalaszentlászló

Village Center at Zalaszentlászló, 1976–1984, by Imre Makovecz. A continuous porch as an extension of the common roof of the social halls links a remodeled abandonned house, and flat roofed strip shops.

Village Center at Zalaszentlászló. Tree trunk columns of the porch are in dialogue with living trees of the courtyard.

Village Center at Zalaszentlászló. A spacious social hall with tree trunk columns is surrounded by small meeting rooms.

activities. Changes of level and views from stairs and second story areas provide a kind of subdued three-dimensional theater. Various activities can occur simultaneously with mutual knowledge but without mutual disturbance. The exposed wood framing and braces of the roof structures and spotty low lighting add to the interest. Husky locally made furniture designed by Janos Horváth seems almost unmovable and gives a sense of permanence. Inside one enters another world, private and protected by the roofs soaring into the shadows. Built by its users, the tragedies and fragments of this place are reconciled in new social and architectural continuities that add their own memories and reminders.

"When the streamers of the May tree fluttered in the wind during the inauguration ceremony at Zalaszentlászló, among the horsemen passing through the crowd, is that certain victory, the 'could have been ...' And, too, when the crowd sings the national anthem, and I see them, the ungainly, fat, deformed Hungarians as they sing, and I know they are my people, regardless of how it happened, regardless of what we have become. Through bitter, stifled tears I see the triumph along with the defeat, for the song illuminates their faces, the what 'could have been' penetrates what is. Through the deformity I can see what is noble on the ugly, servile faces, and what is dignified through the humiliation; through the bad postures I can glimpse the reality of the phrase, 'he could have cut a fine figure of a man'. In this iridescent vision we unite the archetypal image of man, the true meaning of his sadly beautiful life."

The caretaker of the village center at Zalaszentlászló enjoys pulling out a 1981 set of project drawings prepared in the architectural department of the Technical University in Budapest. A flat roofed steel and glass community center was proposed without regard for site, climate or community. The mentality of such a proposal was not only beyond the ability of the village to either build or maintain, it also represented another alienation of local values.

The following year in the 1985 exhibition catalogue Magyar Élö Epítészet, Living Architecture, Makovecz wrote about the role of architecture to mediate the human experience:

"We need a new and free fate here in Central Europe, we need a new life incorporating our traditions and our peculiar history to be able to do what we have to do for our survival in Europe.

"Our houses suggest an ancient, sometimes dark atmosphere. The chatting of people long deceased can be heard from the walls. Our cupolas cover us as the sky. The plaster-work motifs of folk art of our dispersed ethnic group turn into stereoscopic structures. Our ancestors, chased out of our consciousness now push forward to speak to us, to help us to build what we believe to be belonging to this place, and to be authentically ours. We deal with the revival of ruined and deserted villages and little towns and the story – recognitions, finding each other, conflicts, struggle for a national future – must be concentrated in the villages, roofs, halls and rooms, in the material of our houses, building sites, streets. Otherwise the whole thing is pointless."

The goal of recentering communities has taken many forms. The cultural center by Makovecz at Sárospatak, 240 kilometers from Budapest, quickly received international architectural attention when completed in 1982. But it had taken eight years. Sárospatak, named after its muddy stream, was an early center of Calvinism. It became a place of struggle during the darkest days of communism, the time of the so-called "social stabilization". Makovecz recalls the forced amnesia of that time when robot-like information and technological systems with their zero attention spans were substituted for human feelings, when mankind was pushed to forget its primordial origins, mysteries, and freedoms. But his goal was an architecture that could preserve these impulses "against the abyss of time".

Unlike the rural asymmetry of wood and stucco at Zalaszentlászló, the urbane concrete walls with broad slate roofs at Sárospatak are almost perfectly symmetrical. The entrance is frontal. The confrontational forms are almost monumental. Yet the rough whiteness of the limestone aggregate concrete seems to organically grow out of the white plaza. The almost equal proportion of wall to dark tile roof textures retains the visual pattern of Hungarian village houses but at a more urbane scale.

The cultural complex is a joint facility shared with the adjacent high schools. Originally the building was proposed to be earthembraced, swelling out of the ground with roofs floating over bermed walls. Now it emerges with great furrowed eyes piercing out of its own deep architectural shadows. "A friendly dragon with drooping eyes and long sensual lashes, its scaly arms outstretched around a courtyard embracing visitors ... Under its great beetling brows the hooded eyes of the building watch visitors ... a creature that has slunk out of some fairy-tale Transylvanian forest and made its way to slumber in a provincial town square", commented the Architectural Review in 1984.

The Makovecz intention to create "building beings", epüetlévy, is easily perceived in the anthropomorphic suggestions of the pair of central symmetrical tear-drop shaped windows with their projecting eyelash shades of tinted "plexiglas" or "perspex". The deep sculpting of the eyebrow-shaped bows in the roof, and the sweeping underline curve of the cantilever balcony that provides a deep shadow for the entrance underneath, all reinforce the hypnotic centering.

The plan also has the form of some mutant being. The body is the large centered auditorium seating one thousand people

Cultural Center, Sárospatak

Cultural Center at Sárospatak, 1974–1982, by Imre Makovecz. The U-shaped civic plaza is defined by the continuity of building on three sides, centered by the "pair of eyes" balcony, and punctuated by two symbolic columns.

Cultural Center at Sárospatak. Double balcony with projecting "eye-lash" protection is the most obvious detail.

with balconies accessed from the upper floor. On each floor a broad transverse entry hall provides a furnished lobby and gallery that as a civic lounge overlooks the central plaza. Its axis is bound by large windows on each tunnel-like end. The slightly different arms reaching forward contain a cinema on one side and a library on the other, together with a restaurant and a variety of other community spaces.

On the upper floor, concrete columns engaged as part of the wall swell at the top into capitals. Here milled timbers triangulate out and up, treelike, to support the high planar wood ceiling with its exposed beam structure. The dramatic lobby space continues at the ends as a wood barrel vault that burrows to the brilliant light of fully glazed end windows.

On the interior of the auditorium the architect's original concept has been compromised. Structural and aesthetic intentions are truncated and less successful than in the lobby. Branch struts

Cultural Center at Sárospatak. The transverse hall serves both as a circulation spine, and as a civic lobby and lounge.

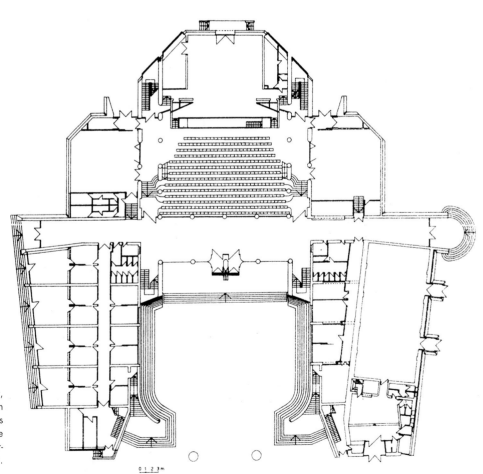

Cultural Center at Sárospatak. Plan of ground floor, revealing anthropomorphic symmetry with main auditorium and stage at the head. Library and offices wing on the left is balanced by the cinema on the right. The extended arms are a transverse hall that overlooks the plaza.

0 1 2 3m

58

rise and curve to shelter the balconies. But a static timber-gridded ceiling rides uncomfortably above. The ends of the grasping arches are empty.

The major outdoor space, the paved plaza, is a forecourt embraced on three sides by the building. Along the sides, outdoor stairs held by sweeping outreaching walls provide access to the upper floor and add to the theater of the plaza. Along the street two celebratory piers mounted by sculptured mythological figures stand as sentries. The two stone figures by László Péterfy embody the principals of darkness and light, the moon and the sun. A man is being lofted away by a gigantic eagle, a "turul". On the other one, a "szkita", a Hungarian mythological elk, rears on his hind legs. Although placed symmetrically, the themes and figures contrast. Their presence add dimensions both human and legendary in the same way that sculpted mythical figures humanize the cool villas of Palladio.

This deliberate and sensitive civic plaza was informed by the plan of the well-built Teacher Training School across the street of 1912 by Jenö Kismarty-Lechner (1878–1962) together with László Warga. Its three-sided grassed yard with two columnar trees as sentinels along the street are mirror-imaged in the Makovecz exterior design that complements and completes the composition. In a 1987 interview with Zoltán Nagy Makovecz has explained:

"The cultural center in Sárospatak is a U-shaped building, opposite to Jenö Lechner's building, in front of which stand two gigantic poplar trees, like two dots on the letter Ü. On the other side of the street, we located two sculptures, each on an 8 meter-tall column, repeating the figure image of the trees. This way, the space in front of the building became more defined like a forum, a gathering place, because that is what it really is. To some extent, we respond to the elements, the trees living across the street; and to some extent my building responded to Lechner's building which represents the last example of the Hungarian national romanticism. Therefore, the relationships between old and new make a unified end result."

Yet this confident architecture came only with great trial and challenge: the design which took four years was followed with uncertainty during construction which took another four years. At the building dedication the cultural anxiety of Makovecz was expressed together with an explanation of cultural spirit:

"'Inner man' is spoiled by rapidly-expanding technology and constant anxiety about the threat of all-out war. Celebration and human dignity is doubtful. I am afraid there is no holding an unbalanced mankind from abandoning civilization. A balance can be preserved only by having a relationship between the inner man and the other orders of creation. The Sárospatak Center ... represents the formal entry of nature and prehistoric culture into our present day."

Cultural Center at Sárospatak. The rectangular auditorium is dominated by the construction of the roof, with angled struts or arms in motion, dynamically reaching up from concrete columns to grasp the static timber grid-frame.

Village Center at Bak, 1985–1988, by Imre Makovecz. Elusive in scale and heavily textured, the building rises amorphously, looming like a giant bird wing.

Village Center, Bak

Similar in social intent, but in complete architectural and urban contrast, the village center at Bak designed by Makovecz in 1985 is a stand-alone object building. Bak is 14 kilometers south of the anonymous new county seat of Zalaegerszeg in southwest Hungary. But there is nothing anonymous about the Makovecz design in an otherwise undistinguished village supported by a large lumber mill, railroad yards, and some agriculture. The theme, spirit, and invisibly, the floor plan, interpret a great eagle.

"Eagle" is the old Hungarian word for a gate post or door frame. Here the entry posts are carved as eagles to frame the doorway. But these eagles also are a reminder of a lost community image of that sacred totemic bird, the "turul", with its allusions to nobility and greatness. As in many Hungarian villages, the Bak memorial to the fallen of World War I was an

60

obelisk with the image of the totemic eagle – an image that had been systematically obliterated or destroyed throughout the country during the communist period. There was no chance that the Bak obelisk and its image could be replaced. Thus the floor plan of the new village center is a symmetrical eagle with great outspread wings. But that abstract bird image is a hidden secret that cannot be seen and thus cannot be banished.

The dedication plaque next to the entrance records Makovecz as architect, Gábor Mezei as interior architect, and Kozsegi Közos Tawács as builder. But like other community centers it was erected not just by local builders. Many local citizens participated. As in traditional villages everywhere people built for themselves. After two years in construction, the opening celebrations were 20–21 August 1988.

With grassed berms covering the walls up to window sills, the building sits somewhat remotely, like a natural or found object. Photographs tend to exaggerate its modest dimensions, the size of two barns. But its presence is monumental if not monstrous. The uncertain building form is amorphously revealed. Uneven weather-blackened boards cover virtually all the exterior and now gather moss. Many swallow nests are lodged in the ragged edges. The waves of boards make uneven layered skirts. The constantly changing planes of individual boards and their grouped ranks are continuously shifting in the sunlight. This animated deep skin is all the more mysterious as roofs merge with walls. Windows seem small and inconsequential. On the exterior the building is all shaggy roof, which fits the village like a characterful barn. It is a very friendly and homely barn for birds. There is no attempt at urban design and no awareness of the exterior space except the entrance at the corner – up a broad flight of stairs to arrive between totemic poles with eagle heads flanking the protective roof. The pair of totemic poles is repeated twice inside where pairs of husky structural poles are yoked to provide bearing for the center of the building.

The friendly interior is both penetrable and spacious, as well as moody. Natural light pierces dramatically throughout. From the entry the dark green-black stained ceiling flows upward into dark vaults. Lower walls and columns are masonry and white. The blackened beams and boarding provide depth and uncertainty to the exposed underside of the roof. Some parts of the interior juxtapose scales with two and three story columns penetrating closely spaced floors. The auditorium with its upstairs balcony is on the right, and the snack bar on the left has a library above. Custom-designed chairs hint at demonic associations. The interior space flows irregularly with its own ambiguous life, strained somewhat by the hidden forms of the plan. The Bak village center seems constantly inhabited, just as the birds are constantly tending their nests outside. Makovecz explained in Magyar Építömüvészet in 1988:

Village Center at Bak. The entrance is guarded by two symbolic gate posts carved as totemic eagles.

Village Center at Bak. From the upper story among the dark exposed roof framing looking down into the bright masonry-walled entry hall.

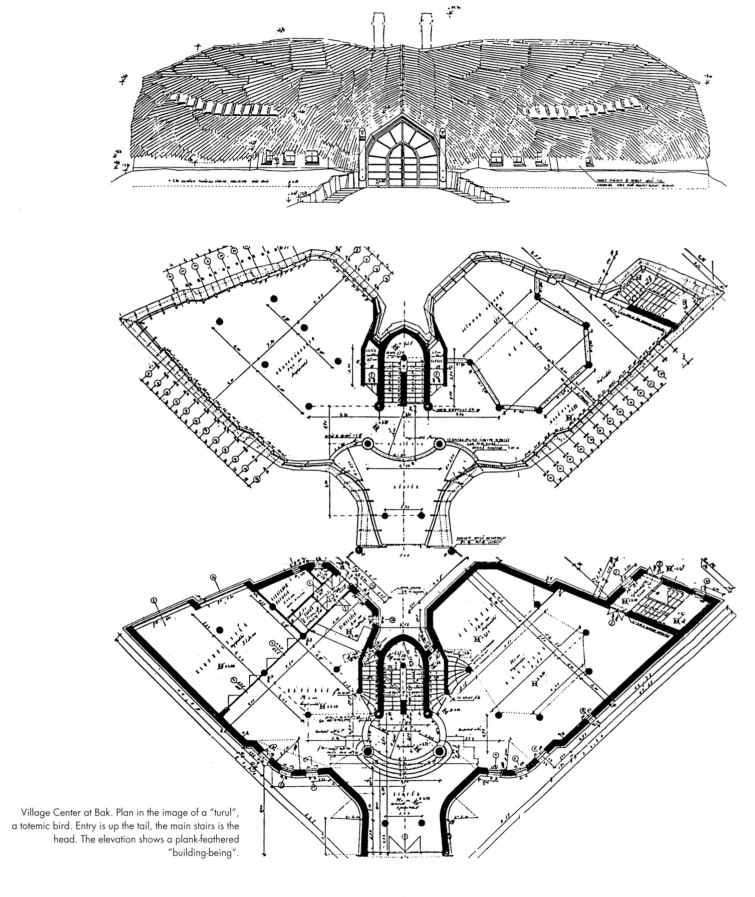

Village Center at Bak. Plan in the image of a "turul", a totemic bird. Entry is up the tail, the main stairs is the head. The elevation shows a plank-feathered "building-being".

"I have done everything I could to help to make nice buildings of local materials, inexpensively, suitable for the use of the village communities. The relationship with the historical and the geological environment is important; so is the material, the theory, and the beauty. But the most important thing is the drama of building."

"The essence of building, I thought, was not the material, the force, the structure or the style, but the drama itself. This thought has become my firm conviction."

Perhaps the most ambitious of the community centers is the Makovecz/Makona scheme of three interlocking timber domes in Szigetvár. Designed already in 1984, it took many years until the building could be completed. An aspiring mayor is credited with the leadership in a backwater town to create a place where he can proudly step out with his wife to a civic function in a distinctive setting. Beyond the ceremonial grandeur of the axial progression, is its sense of spiritual integrity that grows out of structure and organization.

The complex has a symmetrical front on a narrow street – the major road east to Pécs and west to Barcs which was expected to be rerouted to change the town center into a pedestrian zone. A master plan by Makovecz for the whole town identified several sites for a community center. It could have been beside the battlefield, or next to the castle – a fresh beginning – but there was a need to intensify the inner core.

Soft-edged steeples on the street tower 25 meters to frame a forecourt facing south. From this urbane paved plaza, one formally penetrates the first dome on axis, an impressive circulation lobby. The major auditorium fills the second wooden dome, 17 meters high that seems even larger than its 15 meter diameter. The third dome, the stage, continues the aerial interlocking architectural spaces with their curved timber ribs cresting from the top of poured concrete columns.

The constructive theme of masonry walls and columns emerging out of the ground, to be surmounted by an exposed timber superstructure spanning the space is easily understood. It is a constructional analogy to philosophic themes about building as a human activity mediating between earth and sky. Makovecz admits a personal subjective belief that buildings must be heavy and stone-like at the bottom in contrast to growing lightness as they move upwards. From a practical point of view, electric cables, lighting fixtures, and water lines are never placed in the upper wooden parts of the construction. This not only avoids potential leaks and fire in the most vulnerable part of the building, but it provides lighting and environmental services as part of the base platform as a theoretical concept. The aesthetic result is that these buildings are easily sensed in an understandable way, regardless of their particular spatial or material details. Part of this imagery is also the aesthetic tension between

Community Center, Szigetvár

Center at Szigetvár, 1984–1993, by Imre Makovecz. Soft-edged steeples on a major road guard the entrance forecourt.

Community Center at Szigetvár. Closely spaced, thin ribs of soft pine make the domes light and economical to span large spaces.

reversed color fields, where the top of the building is dark and shadowed, and the lower heavy parts are light and bright.

More difficult than the aesthetics at Szigetvár was an ideal organic method of community involvement in construction. A system of local builders guided by a construction manager is preferred to the easy use of a fixed price contract with a large state-operated general contractor. But the limited skills and experience of local workers are often additionally compromised by lack of vision and incentive, or even poor direction and co-ordination. The voluntary participation of local citizens in construction multiplies the challenge. Thus, the architect's office such as Makona is typically an intensely active participant and coordinator of the construction process, not an observer, supervisor or inspector as is typical in the Western countries.

At Szigetvár the project was poorly initiated. The timing of the local authority budget forced a hasty beginning and poor

Community Center at Szigetvár. Copper cladding protects domes of light wood construction. Masonry walls are covered with landscaped earth berms.

craftsmanship, and ended by running out of money. With the main roofs almost finished, the construction site stood idle for two years. The goal of artisan participation that included resolving construction details on the site had backfired. Here the construction process resulted in anger, tensions, accusations, and conflict – an indication of the workers' involvement. Reorganizing and reorienting the process included bus trips for carpenters and bricklayers to see completed organic buildings, to understand potential results of a participative process.

In Hungary the problems with motivation and craftsmanship were a result of low and uniform wages and a guaranteed job, characteristic of socialist policies. The strategy of organic architects to improve this performance has not been the capitalistic one of raising wages in a competition of increased skills, but rather to infuse meaning into the work. Local and ordinary natural materials, such as soft wood, are used to build structures of visible and distinctive quality, all within the local community and the local economy. Both the experience and the tangible result then can continue as a living part of the community. Local workmen should have an enriched idea of the value of local unprocessed materials and lively built examples of the potentials of their own craft. These can be troublesome and exhausting responsibilities for the architect. Such participative roles are not typical for Western architects, where construction is usually considered a quality-control manufacturing process to deliver to a specification, defined by contractual dates and prices. Construction workers in such a process are on-site manufacturing units of productivity.

For Makovecz, architecture is a participative process in the drama of life. All participants must be engaged emotionally as well as physically. And when the building is completed there must be some residual value aside from wages. Unlike the deliberate premeditated design of classical Greek drama, where the audience sang with the chorus, and where the space of the theater was extended through its place within the contours of the land out to the horizon, and where the time of day and season transported the event in a carefully orchestrated synthesis, each emergent Hungarian civic drama is orchestrated extemporaniously. In unknown directions, fresh resolution reconnects people, both reinforcing and creating new culture.

Two other community centers were completed in the 1980s with perhaps less drama either aesthetically or in construction. Both Jászkisér and Jászapati are variations on how to provide a large performance and meeting hall together with some small support spaces within a simple enclosure. Both buildings also offer aesthetic variants on the masonry column, its capital and how the lacy timber superstructure is supported. Makovecz refers to the knotted column capitals as "balványok", trees of life or idols of life.

Community Center at Szigetvár. Concrete walls and columns provide the spring points for curved light wood struts and ribs.

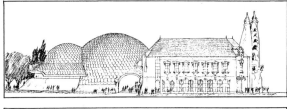

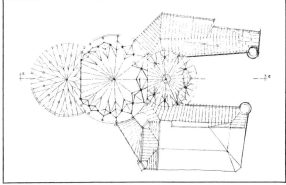

Community Center at Szigetvár. Elevation and sketch plan show remodeling of an existing block to form one side of the entry forecourt which is terminated by two towers. The three domes are aligned on the centerline of the forecourt.

Meeting hall, Ceglédpuszta

Yet another example of architecturally rooting a village is the hall at Bagod, west of Zalaegerszeg. Here a handsome two-century old house was renovated and restored by Imre Makovecz and Zoltán Koppány between 1984 and 1986. Its bright yellow color and substantial forms communicate a reconstructed pride as well as history while providing village facilities.

Probably the smallest gem of a village community center is the tiny 1984–1986 meeting hall at Cegléspuszta by Ervin Nagy, then with Makona. 15 kilometers to the northwest of Szigetvár, this is a village that does not appear on most maps, and there are no road signs. At the end of a long one-lane concrete road is a recent lineal village. At the far end near the general store nestled in a grove of mature chestnut trees is a shadowy wooden hall. Thick double-layered shingle boards follow the bulbous swelling forms of the natural curvature of its timber frame. The single-space interior with its balcony overlook is lined with solid planks. Arched openings are oriented to the four cardinal points. It is a grounded space infused with forest spirits.

Meeting Hall at Cegléspuszta, 1984–1986 by Ervin Nagy of Makona. Thick double-layered shingles provide a continuous skin.

Much more ambitious is the community center at Kakasd midway between Paks and Pécs. Begun in 1986 without adequate funding and still unfinished a decade later, it is slowly being completed, in a way caught on the cusp of political change. A large meeting hall and two large towers are arranged asymmetrically near the highway, with local offices, a tavern, a bank, a local museum, and other spaces. The goal was to link two adjacent villages and to anticipate the rerouting of the highway. Makovecz admits to the slight absurdity of the commission – an unbalanced product of the old socialist regime. Kakasd is a village that itself is in continuous metamorphosis, and an example of patterns of ethnic replacement. A few centuries ago many of the original Hungarians were killed during the Turkish occupation, to be replaced by German-speaking Swabish who were searching for religious freedom. After World War II many of the Swabish were pushed out, to be replaced by Székely refugees from Eastern Transylvania, who made their way west by foot through Yugoslavia.

The project was begun by a Swabian mayor and continued by a Székely mayor. The forms of the design follow a sense of this history. The original plan had a prow-shaped element that projected forward – the Swabians had come rowing down the Danube and then arrived by wagon across the land. But the most visible design elements are the two towers in deliberate dynamic dialogue. With stout bases, and proportioned with great confidence, here are two iconic memories of the villagers origins. The "Germanic" and precise metal-covered bulbous Baroque tower addresses the shaggy wooden textures of a dream church tower from 17th century Transylvania. Old Székelys of the community still remember their church now in ruins in their village in Romania. Some will not live to see this project finished.

Meeting Hall at Ceglédpuszta. This single space hall is in a chestnut grove.

Community Center, Kakasd

Left and right:
Community Center at Kakasd, 1986–1996, by Imre Makovecz. The bulbous tower of the existing orthodox church seen in juxtaposition with the two towers of the new community center.

Makovecz as an architectural priest sees community representation and assembly as multiple forms of spiritual activity that require deliberate design response. To build some of the story of the place and its people is a dramatic performance of private knowledge, of secrets to be revealed and confirmed in architectural experience. Thus past and future are fused in the uncertainty of life by reinforcing self-identity and dignity. Community is shared experience as well as shared roots.

Typically these community centers were new buildings that emerged where no existing facilities were available. But the potential of community use of school facilities opened new possibilities in the late 1980s. The new school gymnasium or Sports Hall in the village of Visegrád next to the Pilis Forest Park north of Budapest is such a project. Initiated by Imre Makovecz in 1985, the design was finalized in 1987, and the building was completed in 1989. Sited next to the village church and the parochial school, it has become a community landmark. Its whiteness contrasts with the pale yellow walls and deep green trim of the nearby Baroque church. Together they make a colorful volumetric statement of village identity beside the Danube. A large shed encloses a large sports hall as well as lockers and meeting rooms within one envelope. The severity of the exterior is surprising. The design is rooted to the ground by low masonry walls of fieldstone with an irregular top. The recessed mortar joints emphasize the naturally textured surfaces. The upper walls at the profile ends become a thin gothicised pattern in plaster and wood. Regular spikes march across the

Sports Hall, Visegrád

Sports Hall at Visegrád. The new hall seen from the highway across a meadow, with the old village church tower and the Pilis Forest hills.

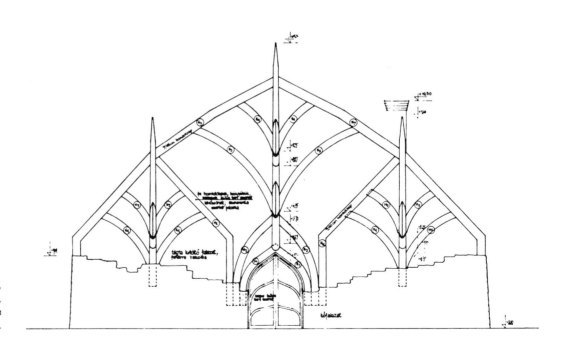

Sports Hall at Visegrád, 1985–1989, by Imre Makovecz. North elevation, showing the timber frame rising out of a new fieldstone wall with a broken top.

Sports Hall at Visegrád. Within a symmetrical space the asymmetrical row of columns only on one side provides structural bracing, and defines the seating area.

Sports Hall at Visegrád. Main entrance.

Secondary School, Fonyód

ridge of the bowed gable roof as lightening rods marking the structural bays.

The interior reveals this pattern of structural regularity in curved structural supports and braces that reduce the roof span, and shape its arched asymmetry. Interior columns are dynamically used only on one side of the space. The balcony bleachers placed over the dressing and meeting rooms add to the impact of this off-center singular interior space.

This major shift in the concept of community centers was early represented in the extension and remodeling of the Secondary School of Fonyód, a town on the shores of Lake Balaton. The 1986 design completed in 1989 by Ferenc Salamin was a large job entrusted to one of the young new generation of architects who had come through the Visegrád Workshops and a Makona apprenticeship.

The old flat-roofed modern International Style school building was almost the focus of the town at the end of a broad street leading back from the lake and the railroad station. The addition of a large meeting hall for public as well as school uses brought the building functionally into the community. Other ad-

Extension and Remodeling Secondary School at Fonyód, 1986–1989, by Ferenc Salamin of Makona. Although the school is now larger, the remodeling has brought the roof down to be more in scale with the town center.

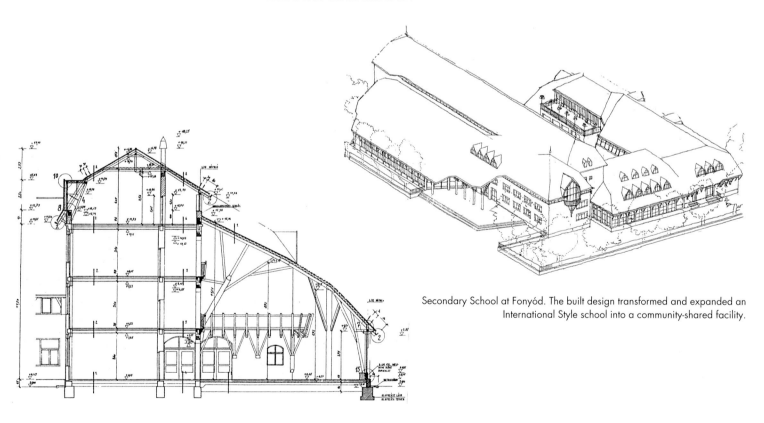

Secondary School at Fonyód. The built design transformed and expanded an International Style school into a community-shared facility.

Secondary School at Fonyód. Section. The new assembly hall on the right, on the left the old flat-roofed school that received another floor and a new roof.

ditions and modifications transformed it into a characterful building of hooded slate roofs, dormers, and gables and dissolved the sterility of this factory for learning.

The impressive meeting hall holding 500 people is especially dramatic. A three-story white masonry side wall with arched opening provides balcony overlooks and a pierced transition to the walls of the old school. It also provides structural support for sloped columns that branch into timber struts supporting the exposed rafters and deck of the new roof. Along the other side and on the ends, continuous windows bring in daylight and relate the space to the town outside. Almost symmetrical in plan but asymmetrical in section, the addition ties back into the massing of the old school. The meeting hall design is an enlargement and refinement of the enclosed Jászkisér hall, but now opened up to natural light and the community.

The new Arpad Vezer School (Technical High School) at Sárospatak completed in 1993 by Imre Makovecz provides a fresh idea of community generated by an educational and social nucleus primarily for school population aged 14 to 18. It uses a symmetrical and conventional planning scheme to organize a complex of larger halls and smaller classrooms within a whole of easily identifiable parts. Here husky pointed steeples terminate the four corners guarding the exposed ends. It is a set of lower towers in a town with major steeples of both Calvinist and Catholic churches. But perhaps the four corner towers are also a memory of the four short towers on the corners of the medieval Sárospatak Castle of the Rákosi.

Makovecz suggests that the architectural concept is "primitive". He recalls his meeting with the teachers before designing the new school. He asked, "What do you most hate about school buildings?" He wrote down the replies: "Classrooms in a row". "Double loaded corridors." "All the teachers in a single teacher's staff room." When he asked them to draw their ideal school on paper it was a square, or an open space with classrooms around the sides. That is the concept at Sárospatak.

Everyone entering the school comes into a four-story skylit hall, the aula. This major entry experience is both assembly auditorium and circulation center, "filled with the everyday spiritual needs of the school". Concrete columns grow out of the ground. Their tops develop feathered wings that are arms serving as a balcony rail. Stylized concrete heads and faces as capitals provide the structural transition to curved wood ribs that branch upward like flying hair to support the large wood-decked hip roof that breaks open along the centerline with a continuous skylight. But the focus of the space is the symmetrical stairway at the end which serves as podium and stage for assembly. Concrete wings unfold to protect the rising stairs and center the experience. In profile their feathered edges also be-

Secondary School at Fonyód. The large daylit assembly hall was built along the wall of the old school; the exposed wood roof structure is the only decorative element.

Arpad Vezer School, Sárospatak

Arpad Vezer School at Sárospatak, 1989–1993, by Imre Makovecz. The planes of dark roof slates are lifted to reveal the intricacy of window details and angled timber roof supports of the large sports hall.

Arpad Vezer School at Sárospatak. The flatness of the classroom wing is set in motion by paint patterns and window shape. Depth is given by the deep overhang and exposed timber struts of the top floor.

Arpad Vezer School at Sárospatak. The school is centered by a large entry and assembly hall. It is skylit, columned and balconied, with focus provided by a processional stair.

Arpad Vezer School at Sárospatak. Balconied towers containing meeting rooms symmetrically guard the entrance.

come stylized fir tree silhouettes. It is a feat of this architecture that everyone on that stairs feels special.

The overlooking balconies are terminated by small rooms, teachers at one end, students at the other, with other service spaces that when stacked become not just the ends of the circulation system but the towers expressed on the outside. The level of craftsmanship is high, and everything is strong and smooth. The marble tile floor of the entry hall, the carefully bush-hammered concrete surfaces on stairs, and the continuous exterior shingles give a sense of confidence and repose. Although construction was halted because of lack of funds it was finally completed for dedication in September 1993.

Similarly the large educational and social center at Csenger is a regionally supported complex, in addition to immediate local participation. This community at the far east of the Great Plain, next to Romania and not far from the Ukrainian border had little new building in the past few generations because of its proximity to these frontiers. Earlier it was an important market town servng parts of Transylvania that are now in Romania. Indeed, the last major building was the handsome Reform Church begun in the 13th century in the same block. The shift in political climate in the late 1980s as well as a new national agenda of development initiated a large regional school. Old buildings were remodeled and large new ones were planned such as the Sports Hall of 1987–1992 and the Restaurant Refectory of 1989–1993. Now this remote village has become a major architectural mecca to the credit of local political leadership in collaboration with the architects Makovecz and Makona.

The first major architectural event as one drives into the village is the deeply covered porch of the Csenger Elementary School. A single white column supports the fans of timber struts that carry the red tiled expanses of roof. Small lunette dormers lifting from the roof give eyes to a certain anthropomorphic image. White walls articulated with engaged columns and windows quietly provide continuity along the street line.

The Csenger Elementary School and Community Hall by Lörinc Csernyus of Makona completed in 1992 contains one of the finest new interior spaces in Hungary. A continuous shaped skylight floats over the king post trussing of the timber roof framing. But it is the dynamic placement of the columns that energizes the essentially triangular space. One side has the columns planned in a straight line while on the other their plan positions are curved. Then as the poured-in-place concrete columns rise, they move forward reaching up with unfolded capitals to clasp the spreading timbers of the roof trussing. A continuous balcony, stairs at the end, and a terracing of the ground floor all add to the spatial dynamic. But it is the natural light from the sides and above that vitalizes the space.

Elementary School, Csenger

Elementary School and Community Hall at Csenger, 1987–1992, by Lörinc Csernyus of Makona. The main entrance on the corner is emphasized by a single stout column that branches many struts to raise the roof to a protective canopy. In the background is the Sports Hall.

Elementary School and Community Hall at Csenger. A skylit assembly hall is defined by balcony access to classrooms on three sides. The slightly curved plan and the leaning columns create a dynamic space.

Elementary School and Community Hall at Csenger. Balcony access to classrooms.

Elementary School and Community Hall at Csenger. During construction the new leaning columns await the construction of the trussed skylit roof. In the background the brick 13th century Reform Church.

Elementary School and Community Hall at Csenger. The single column under the entry porch with its branching roof struts provides a visual pivot.

Elementary School and Community Hall at Csenger. The principle public entrance to the community hall of the school is on the corner as one enters the village. Classroom wings define the streets.

Sports Hall, Csenger

The Csenger Sports Hall designed by László Vincze of Axis studio represents a shifted architectural vision. Aggressive and not so soft as earlier organic community centers, it still uses natural light and some familiar building materials. The continuous ridge skylight is especially effective in daylighting the arena. But the scale and detailing of the building and its colors, make it seem remote from Hungarian organic ideals with their typical images of red tile roofs and white walls. Here a green shingled roof is quieter and softens the bulk of a large mass. But the salmon-colored brick walls have an industrial and foreign air, although chosen to match the ancient brick of the 13th century Reform church. The inclusion of more industrialized materials such as the exposed brick in walls and piers, and the tension rods for the roof construction represent an increase in the availability of manufactured materials. The tie rod and timber roof structure is both medieval in precedent, and late modern in its economy. Severity and large scale bring a hardness quite different from the soft forms, modest scale and familiar materials associated with Hungarian organic architecture.

For Makovecz the old period of community centers is over. Villages are now finding themselves as an entity and a community without outside professional services. Curiously, when translated the words "a müvelödés háza" or "faluház" sometimes appear as "house of culture" or "civic center". In all Eastern Europe such words usually defined official centralization and political formalization controlled by the system. That authoritarian

Sports Hall at Csenger, 1989–1992 by László Vincze of Makona. The deliberate difference in design and scale with the adjacent school is emphasized by both its independent site and distinct choice of materials.

Sports Hall at Csenger. The facade visibly incorporates the ends of traverse tension ties with their cross-shaped plates. In spite of the playful corrugated edge to the roof at the protected entrance, the crisp details of materials reveal a certain hardness.

Sports Hall at Csenger. Daylight enters from all sides and adds to the lightness of the economical roof construction.

practice is the opposite of these Hungarian grass roots origins as social but anti-authority places, locally organized and of the community. Now that era is finished and once forbidden rights to freely socialize exist again. As each club and special interest association begins to find its own place, the participatory process of local interaction must find new media.

As Makovecz said in 1988 in Magyar Építömüvészet: "A new network has been created in the country, truly new; with a new spirit behind it. The agitative and propagandistic network of this new spirit has come into being in a place where nothing had been before. Blood began to refill into new veins".

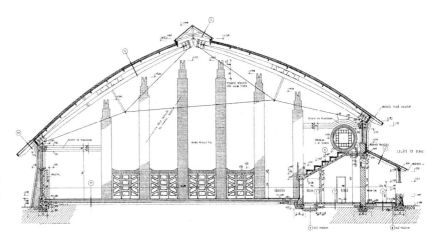

Sports Hall at Csenger. Section, showing thin timber vaults held in compression by triangulated tension cables. The whole light-weight assembly is continuously raised on one side to provide clearance for the bleechers with the dressing rooms underneath.

Hospitality and Recreation

Beyond the Pécs Group

Youth Club House in Balokányi Park at Pécs, 1972, by Peter Oltai of the Pécs Group. With its decorative color and ornamental form, this structure contrasted with the anonymous prefabricated housing and workplaces of daily life.

Youth Club House at Pécs. Although structure is expressed, the cantilevered balcony, the interior faceted globe under the skylight and the undisturbed symmetry suggest a floating autonomous space.

Before the Pécs Group as a professional studio was disbanded in 1975 by the state planning office, Baranyaterv, the Young Studio had dispersed its seeds. Already successful and convincing designs had been constructed and had received strong, if unofficial local support. Built ideas had demonstrated the new architecture not just as a refreshing incident but as a preferable alternative. Typically new architectural ideas are never initiated anywhere by a monolithic authority. Rather, new design directions are shown by adventurous professionals for private clients, for a social elite, or for a self-selected leadership within a specific sector of the religious, financial or political realm. But in Hungary in the 1970s, designs for social and hospitality purposes initiated the spread of organic ideas for a general public.

Typically functional needs outside of official architecture and beyond the restrictions of prefabricated housing or factories allowed buildings of distinctive quality and the exploration of new forms. Thus it was not post offices, state ministries, party headquarters or the like that permitted and encouraged a fresh vitality and originality. It was buildings like clubhouses, recreation structures, and vacation hotels, guided by new concepts of place and identity, that formed a social architecture of a different sort.

Among the early completed buildings of the Pécs Group was the 1972 Youth Club House in the Balokányi Park in Pécs. Designed by Péter Oltai, it is primarily an octagon social hall with a raised or pent roof. A flat roofed one story service bustle of kitchen and toilets extends on the backside. The symmetrical exterior of the hall gives no hint of entrance and its modest scale is illusive. Its globe-like form is simultaneously heavy and weightless. Deep green, yellow, and red glazed wall tiles attach the building to the land and to the seasons, and identify it with the colorful cultural presence of the famous Zsolnay ceramic factory not far away. On the other hand the tapered skinny columns hardly attach the polychrome planar ball to the ground. The crystal top and the transparent portholes on the sides add to this unreality. In its color and its form this fantasy could only be in Pécs.

The interior is primarily a high open circular hall with a well-detailed wood balcony. The flower-like radiating wood roof trusses are exposed. Illumination by a central crystal skylight reinforces the enclosed form and the centralizing vertical axis common in early organic designs. In a search for ethnic identity the self-referential circular plan was preferred, and precedents in history and prehistory were sought. Thus, such early circular Christian structures as the 13th century Romanesque chapel at Kallósd in Zala county on an earlier foundation, and the 13th century Körtemplom, the hexagon chapel in a cylinder at Kiszombor east of Szeged were admired as possibly derived from earlier pre-Christian Asian prototypes such as yurts. There was a consciousness of the forms of mutual self-support and protection as exemplified by other cultures, such as the traditional wagon circle of pioneers in the Great Plains of the USA or the symbolic circle of teepees in the annual encampments of the American Plains Indians.

In the company Resort Hotel completed by 1977 at Fadd-Dombori, the architect Tibor Jankovics of the Pécs Group provided a large hospitality complex with a distinct low profile in the flat countryside near the Danube River. Around the perimeter the protective red-tiled roof reaches almost to the ground.

Youth Club House at Pécs. Support functions such as toilets and kitchen are located in a service circle with its own crystal-like skylight to allow the circular club hall to retain its integrity.

Resort Hotel, Fadd-Dombori

Resort Hotel at Fadd-Dombori, 1977, by Tibor Jankovics of the Pécs Group. A perimeter of hotel rooms encloses the recreation space.

Circular hoods provide openings, in a scale suitable to a large rural structure. A single round gate between buildings emphasizes the security of closure and privacy. Inside the courtyard the structural grid steps forward in plan to provide appropriate public interior spaces, as well as to define sheltered outdoor patios and terraces. The hotel rooms in two stories around the perimeter with balcony access provide an encircling enclosure.

Resort Hotel at Fadd-Dombori.

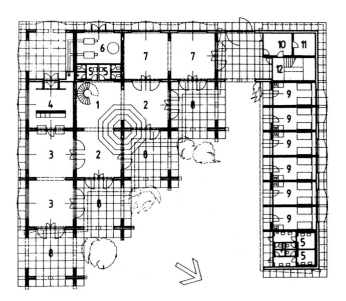

Resort Hotel at Fadd-Dombori. Ground floor plan and section.

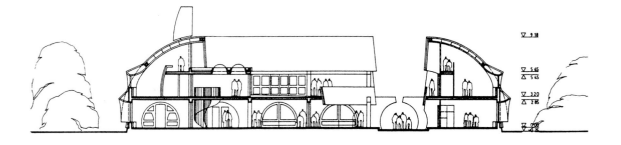

By 1978 Jankovics had opened his own office, Formaterv, and moved to Keszthely. Here he completed the Hotel Fönis, Phoenix Hotel, by 1984 which was named after the first pleasure yacht in Lake Balaton. A remodeled one story resort built on marshy land near Lake Balaton, the exterior is modest. The plan consists of four low wings of hotel bedrooms attached to a large central hall that contains lobby, reception and other public functions. For economy in foundations there are only two large masonry free-standing columns in the central hall. Timber braces reach out to support the continuous roof girders that run the length of the hall. As a capital on top of the columns, a nest of stacked finished wood conceals structural connections and shields indirect lighting. The columns become sculptural focal elements internalizing the space where there is no exterior view.

The hotel sleeping rooms were custom-designed by Ildikó Csete with neat built-in furniture to maximize their modest dimensions. They are characterized by spare lines and the use of natural wood and custom silkscreen printed fabrics.

In 1975, the young architect Sándor Dévényi returned to his hometown Pécs. After six years in the only professional program in the country he graduated from the Technical University in Budapest in 1973 and then worked for two years for the state design office, Iparterv, but became homesick. Born in 1948 he was more than a decade younger than the members of the Pécs Group. He returned after their studio was disbanded to develop his own career independently. Although practicing in the same city, Dévényi developed a very distinct organic discipline, quite separate from the pioneering Pécs Group.

Dévényi first worked for the state planning office, Baranyaterv. Such a combined architectural engineering design and development company offered unusual opportunities for its small number of architects. One job was to rectify ground subsidence within Pécs. This 2000-year-old city has a labyrinth of underground tunnels, and limestone caves used for wine storage which were beginning to collapse. A brick vaulting system was initiated to provide structural stability and the underground spaces were proposed for various social purposes. A nightclub, the University Cellar Club initiated between 1976 and 1985 has yet to be completed. However, the interesting underground Aquarium Terrarium (1983–93) has been an instant popular success in its re-use of old tunnels and caves under the city.

Another civic project was the historic reconstruction of the Tannery at No. 9 Felsömalom or Upper Mill Street between 1976–84 which was adapted as the museum of the city of Pécs and the history of the labor movement, Várostörténeti. Tanneries had existed in Pécs since the 15th century. This was a 1773 building, originally one story with a drying attic under the roof. A 1788 large wing addition was followed by 19th

Phoenix Hotel, Keszthely

Phoenix Hotel at Keszthely, 1984, by Tibor Jankovics. A curved garden wall, natural materials, and a patio combined with entrance helped to enliven the remodeling of a modest hotel.

Phoenix Hotel at Keszthely. The roof of the lobby is supported with just two columns. The column capitals are nests of layered sticks that conceal structural connections and provide indirect artificial lighting.

University Cellar Club at Pécs, 1984, by Sándor Dévényi. The structural necessity to support collapsing tunnels is met by brickwork in lively patterns that transform the space.

and 20th century modifications including use as a restaurant, tavern, and a dance hall. Dévényi achieved a creative adaptation of the few remaining parts of the earliest historic fabric for a new use. The ground floor arches were glazed, and then stone window frames similar to historical examples nearby were hung suspended in the center in front of the glass, a reminder, as it were, of the multiple lives of the building. On the interior the original brick vaulting and piers were repaired and exposed. But a new floor and entrance doorway are clearly late 20th century.

Dévényi recalls that "between 1978 and 1980 it became obvious that Baranyaterv and Pécsiterv, the South Trans Danube Designing Enterprise needed a young studio such as the Pécs Group or its equivalent. Free architectural thinking and the new things it gave rise to were missing in such a big company. I would say that they needed a court jester, and that was why they employed me. They needed a joker who makes the palette more colorful; who can be pointed at – 'Look! He belongs to us because we are such a great firm'". In 1980, Dévényi moved from Baranyaterv into Pécsiterv, the Planning Company of South Transdanubia.

He would work 42 hours weekly and then go home to work after hours on small projects trying to establish a private practice. Within Pécsiterv, the largest architectural and engineering office in the region with over 300 employees, most were engineers involved in large-scale heavy construction, industrial development and road design. There were only three architectural studios, and Dévényi was assigned as chief designer to the studio headed by István Kistelegdi, the only member of the Pécs Group remaining in a collective office.

Among their critical early engagements was the urban design of a Pécs roadway bypass. Vak Bottyán, the new motorway near the center of the old city threatened to sever the south-facing slopes of Mecsek Mountain from the urban core. Almost too late and after many buildings had been demolished did they prevail. A tunnel was finally allowed in addition to bridges and changes of grade to maintain both physical and visual linkages. A promenade along Aradi Vértanúk Street overlooking the cathedral, new pedestrian routes, and a strong landscape scheme were among the organic interventions. As far as detailing went, patterns of sequentially unfolding forms typical of the imagery of emerging organic architecture enriched a retaining wall. It was made by stepping the separate boards of the formwork before the concrete was poured into it.

Perhaps because of the boldness of his design skill Dévényi worked for several years conceiving many proposals but not getting any projects built. The first one completed was a honeymoon hotel called the Wedding Hotel or the House of Joy,

Tannery Reconstruction at Pécs, 1976–1984, by Sándor Dévényi. The newly cobble stoned courtyard contrasts with the stuccoed brick arches with their flush frameless glazing.

Tannery Reconstruction at Pécs. Exposed original brick vaults, a new brick floor and triangulated steel doors define the museum space.

Tannery Reconstruction at Pécs. Steel supports cantilevered from the floor suspend small stone window frames.

Formwork on concrete retaining wall along Aradi Vértanúk, a fast bypass road at Pécs, 1979, by Sándor Dévényi.

designed in the summer of 1982 and constructed between 1983 and 1985. Located at 2 Hunyadi Street just up the hill from the main square and the municipal wedding hall at Pécs, the Wedding Hotel could easily be missed: its general color and form match the massing and texture of the surrounding historic city. Its two stories became three because of the slope of the hill, and the familiar steep red tiled roof with projecting dormers allowed a fourth inside the high attic. The irregular site also allowed balconies on the south side and an outdoor patio, overlooking the city. A pizza parlor, photography studio, florist, bakery, and other small shops at ground level make for a mixed commercial use for the private investors and provide conveniences for the newly-weds.

Wedding Hotel, Pécs

Wedding Hotel at Pécs, 1982–1985, by Sándor Dévényi. The details respect both construction materials and the basic massing of the brick bearing walls and timber frames roof.

Wedding Hotel at Pécs. Articulated brick piers turn into scrolls above the roof, crowned by a spikey finial. Wrought iron balcony rails reflect the curve.

Wedding Hotel at Pécs. Wrought iron balustrades and stair rails lead to the bridal suites in the attic.

The picturesque detailing of the Wedding Hotel was not historic but inspired by bridal happiness and youthful exuberance. The richly modeled openings and wall surfaces were based on the brick module. The decorative styles change from rectangular to stepped to sweeping curves and arches, according to the facade and with various qualities of humor. Stepped windows, angled dormers and picturesque chimneys add to the wonderful eclectic diversity of this playfulness. The architectural fun continues inside where elegant sinuous stair rails lead up to the reception space on the third floor, and the lobby continues up into the roof space as balcony access to the secretive attic rooms and bridal suites with dormer windows under the roof.

Dévényi finally opened his own office full-time in Pécs in 1989. He has a particular affection for his hometown and its Mediterranean spirit. Although over 300 kilometers from the Adriatic, Pécs has always enjoyed a benign southern disposition that Dévényi identifies as a special role in Hungary – not so much in terms of politics or economics but as a view of life developed in a particular climate and topography. Those human attitudes apparently originated with the Romans who founded the city as Sopianae, the capital of Eastern Pannonia. Its relaxed character and zest for life strongly survived Turkish and German occupations and persists also in today's prosperity.

Dévényi has an uncomplicated sense of the Hungarian roots in his architecture. He, like all Hungarians, appreciates their independent Asiatic origins from the openness of the great plains of Asia. As a small nation and an ethnic entity totally unrelated to their neighbors, Hungary's need to maintain autonomy and to enhance identity has been ever-present.

But Dévényi finds less inspiration in ancient roots, or in the religious past or in traditional folklore than he does in being European with a unique regional background. Both in his brief descriptions of his own designs as well as in a subjective examination of his works one can detect an eclectic fusion – Turkish, Tartar, and Transylvanian glimpses synthesized with childhood fairy-tale images and the whole diverse architectural imagery of European cultures. His own elegant script lettering is an expressive calligraphic connection with courtly Hungarian history. His distinctive working drawings are exquisite compositions of precise information and lyric lettering. In parallel, his skillful architecture is sometimes pure fantasy and sometimes intellectually sophisticated, always with a Baroque liveliness. When asked why his organic designs work so well in urban settings he finds no conflict – the city is an organic entity in which growth and change are conceptual. Similarly, Dévényi is organically rooted in his own city and region. His architecture communicates that natural integrity with independent artistic energy.

Already in 1981 the Museum of Finnish Architecture and the Alvar Aalto Museum in Helsinki presented nine architects in "Tradition and Metaphor: A New Wave in Hungarian Architecture"; they had assembled the key figures (although Dévényi was not included) but did not identify them as a cohesive movement. Another exhibition, Építészeti: Tendenciák Magyarországon, Hungarian Directions 1968–1981, was held at the Óbuda Gallery and received international acknowledgement as well. The British magazine Architectural Review of June 1982 reported on the show and its warnings against Postmodern plagiarism: "After 20 years of soulless, high-rise, prefab reductive Modernism led by the construction industry with the architect as technical dogsbody, Makovecz believes that Hungarian architects must overcome an ingrained inferiority complex – 'The lack of *Hungarian* architecture is not due to the

Temporary Exhibition Pavilion at Budapest, 1985, by Zoltán Koppány. A summer tent was created from canvas on a light wood frame raised off the ground on short legs and sled runners.

Temporary Exhibition Pavilion at Budapest. Canvas brought a particular quality of daylight to the display of drawings and photographs mounted on wing-shaped fins.

one-sidedness of the construction industry but to the lack of that natural internal force which I have indicated by the two phrases: human dignity and Hungarian identity.'"

At home, public recognition of the new Hungarian architecture as something more than several eccentric architects came late. The opportunity was the summer National Agricultural Fair in Budapest in August 1985. Perhaps there was a correctness that organic architects would exhibit with the products of farmers. They called it Magyar Élö Építészet, Hungarian Living Architecture, using the old Hungarian word for "life", elö, thus perhaps implying that other architecture must not be alive. The catalog's telltale subtitle was Elsö Hazai Kiállitása, the "first exhibition in the home country". For this debut the architectural ideas of Csete and the Pécs Group, and of Makovecz and Makona as well as newcomers like Sándor Dévényi were shown as contributing parts of the larger organic whole. This was no longer a series of new waves, but a comprehensive tide.

Hungarian creative qualities informed the 1985 Temporary Exhibition Pavilion itself, designed by Zoltán Koppány, for this first comprehensive presentation of Hungarian organic architecture in the country. The temporary exhibit gallery was a billowing cloth tent, a white light modulator catching the sun and the dappled shadows of leaves to illuminate photographs and drawings mounted inside on white wing-shaped fins. The structure was raised above the ground, floating above wooden sled rails. The clarity and innocence of this sophisticated white apparition was unusually poetic in proclaiming a broadly-founded movement.

Already many one-man exhibitions had added to the public and professional exposure of these ideas in the previous decade. Other architects never strongly identified with the organic movement nevertheless produced designs that appeared to expand its popularity.

Cattleherd Inn, Balaton Szentgyörgy

Especially adventurous in spirit was the touristic Cattleherd Inn, Gulya Csárda, designed through Forma in 1985 and completed in 1990 at Balaton Szentgyörgy near Keszthely. With conceptual design by György Csete, design development by Gábor Sánta, structural design by Jenö Dulánszky and assistance by Imre Koppány it was a creative team involving two of the original Pécs Group.

The Cattleherd Inn is intended to stop tourist traffic and to provide restaurant and café facilities with a gift shop in the open marshland near the end of Lake Balaton. Based on popular Hungarian interest in their own cowboy culture, the theme focuses on a local herd of the archaic grey cattle kept as an attraction. The owners and sponsors are the South Balaton Agricultural Association. The design is based on images of ancient nomadic cattle culture as fused with star gazing and fantasy elements; a latter-day cluster of stupas seems to have materialized on the lowland.

Cattleherd Inn at Balaton Szentgyörgy, 1985–1990, by György Csete and Gábor Sánta of FORMA. Curved red-tile roofs and a bullet-shaped white brick tower are the distinctive features of this roadside restaurant.

As seen from a fast highway, the building reads with a distinctive profile: Broad tents of red tile sit on a green plain. A circular earth work separates the building from the cattle pasture. The building with its four-square plan is oriented at 45° to the cardinal points and is centered by a white brick tower, part horn, part spaceship. Broad wooden outdoor stairs invite one to take possession of the roof, to climb up the spiral stairs and to look out through the circular holes into the sky.

On the interior the central circular tower of white brick provides an inner sanctum. A wool felt hanging is pulled aside to enter a circular tribal assembly space with a traditional beehive stove placed off-center. Its design with an Orion star pattern is a miniature variation of the larger room and the horn or spaceship on the roof.

Cattleherd Inn at Balaton Szentgyörgy.

Cattleherd Inn at Balaton Szentgyörgy. The tiled roofs go to the ground, a stepped ramp provides access to the roof.

The interior of each of the four quadrants is naturally lit by a sky crystal at its apex, in addition to corner windows. The strong sense of enclosure and protection avoids claustrophobia by an almost sacred quality of light. Painted diamond-shaped sheets on the overhead surfaces provide a sense of continuity and weightlessness. Deliberately a material of potentially anonymous industrial origins is detailed to give character. Custom-designed fabrics including table cloths by Ildikó Csete add to the distinction of the interior.

The high water table discouraged construction of sun-dried mud brick, or adobe, as originally intended. It would also have been easy and in character to use thatch roofs since reeds grow nearby in Lake Balaton and the traditional roofing craft continues. Yet thatched roofs might have been more obvious and therefore less visible. However one reads this curious

Cattleherd Inn at Balaton Szentgyörgy. The restaurant room inside the tent form is lit by daylight from discrete sources.

Cattleherd Inn at Balaton Szentgyörgy. Under the tower, a wool felt hanging is raised to reveal a traditional Hungarian brick beehive stove with an Orion star pattern.

design, it represents a cultural transaction; a dialogue of private and very native thoughts directed toward naive visitors. The visitors like it.

Already by the late 1980s, organic design with its suggestive allusions to other times and places, and especially its statements of renewed Hungarianness became increasingly accepted. The aesthetic richness was added to a broad spectrum of architectural effects, from light and space to the texture of materials. Especially in new buildings around Lake Balaton with its heavy influx of non-Hungarian summer tourists, the distinctive qualities of organic design were encouraged. In the extensive architectural group practice in Keszthely that included Tibor Jankovics under "Forma", organic design became almost mainstream. Large civic commissions as well as many private works such as shops and tourist hotels provided continuous opportunities.

Already in the last work of András Erdei (1946–1986), the large 1986 Swimming Pool at the Resort Hotel in Héviz near Keszthely, a prototypical design had been enlivened by organic imagery with its tree-of-life facade. Erdei wrote:

"Since the mentality of folklore like that of very ancient and natural arts is organic, our architecture could learn a lot from folk art. In Hungary, the task of our organic architecture is to cultivate and spread the organic mode of thinking, and, with the multiplicity of realized buildings, to prove that even in limited and tightly controlled architectural conditions, it is still possible to achieve a humanistic environment."

Similarly the comprehensive development of BM Gyógyintézet, BM Sanatorium, at Héviz by Tibor Jankovics with Nándor Kruppa, István Fehér, Beáta Lukács, and others between 1984 and 1991 involved a handsome new therapy pool. Remodeling and additions help to mend and transform disparate elements built through the years. The free handling of daylight in all the new work brightened and vitalized a large rambling health institution. In the new therapy pool the detailing of clouds of overhead wood grilles conceal the large overhead air handling equipment above the pool. The elegant exposed timber structure of laminated bents with exposed wood purloins and decking reveals the warmth of organic sensibilities without a brash form vocabulary.

Thus for some, the distinctness of organic architectural practice became almost invisible. It had become integral and interchangeable with sensitive and appropriate design. Especially in Pécs but increasingly in Keszthely new designs throughout the community were informed by organic ideas, simply as part of cultural continuity. It was not necessary to make a fresh or challenging statement. Although the design skills of architects such as Dévényi, Kistelegdi, and Jankovics can be found in many small hotels, street furniture, or remodeled shops, other

Sanatorium, Héviz

BM Sanatorium and Therapy Pool at Héviz, 1984–1991, by Tibor Jankovics and Beáta Lukács of FORMA. Old buildings and new construction are organically fused in the courtyard entry.

BM Sanatorium and Therapy Pool at Héviz. A new treatment pool is economically enclosed with laminated beams, and light wood purlins and deck. Lattice clouds conceal mechanical air handling equipment.

designers increasingly participated in the organic transformation of these cities.

The 1991 Gösser Sörkent became the most successful Beer Garden in the resort town of Keszthely. It was designed by Tibor Jankovics with Gyula Balla, János Tóth, and László Tóth as part of the comprehensive practice "Forma". Architectural enclosure using timber sheds and tile roofs were fused with planters held up by clusters of broken rock under a canopy of trees. Living things interlocked with living architecture. The natural and built environments merged in this outdoor architecture of hospitality that may inspire organic architecture to increasingly embrace the worlds of nature.

Gösser Beer Garden at Keszthely, 1991, by Tibor Jankovics of FORMA. Natural materials and living plants provide the setting for outdoor carousing.

Roof as Shelter

The House and Hajlék

Hajlék was the title of the December 1987 exhibition and catalog of the former Pécs Group held at the Budapest Gallery in Budapest. It illustrated concepts of personal "shelter" and "dwelling" with built designs now dispersed throughout Hungary. It underlined the issue of the private and personal house as an architectural statement, and it emphasized the roof as a critical aspect of all organic architecture. In the catalog György Csete explained:

"Hajlék" is one of the most ancient and beautiful Hungarian words. It means more than "shelter". It is derived from the bending of a branch, the curve of a bough, the bow. The space shaped by these sheltering and forceful forms means home."

"The beauty of the word is poetic. It means love and radiating protection. The sound of the word is musical. 'A branch with leaves shall bend a tent', writes László Nagy in the Green Tent Allegory.

"In the word 'Hajlék' is the shelter of light, of love, and of life. In the new Hungarian organic architecture this form of shelter is like the form of all ancient shelters. It is epitomized in the buildings of Makovecz and the works of the architects of Pécs. In these designs the mass of the form has a roundness that contains a budding force. The silhouette resembles the latent energy of trees, haystacks, and hills."

For millennia the concept of protective shelter as illustrated by cupped hands, embracing arms or bowed branches seems to have been part of Hungarian culture. These ideas were always bound in the use of earthy materials, adobe or stone walls, tree timbers and thatch roofs. They were also expressed both graphic and poetic in the 1973 display "Only From Pure Sources" of the Pécs Group. As explained previously, the manifesto explored in detail the relation between the earth and the house.

"The home of man and its transformations: From an earthen dug form through careful crafting into a sterile industrial product. The internal order of the home has two poles along a hypotenuse:

The Fireplace – the source of warmth and light, the working corner, and the serving unit; The Sacred pit – the location of rest, of deep thinking and meditation, of dining, of information. The house structure spans between these two poles, providing the human necessities of sleeping; and the layers of storage." (Plate 25)

Yet the revival of folk houses or the invention of a new rural style was not the intention of the Pécs Group or the other pioneers of organic architecture. Rather they used indigenous traditions as an analogy, as a method of thinking to return public architecture to its natural roots, to its earliest essence. Native language was another source of cultural meaning especially in primal origins. Imre Makovecz was quite articulate in a 1984 essay illustrated by his built works to show how the ancient words of the art of building and their profound meaning could inform the organic architecture of the 20th century.

"Like many other things houses embody the spiritual bond between man and the world. And as a man has defined his stand in life, he personified himself with his house."

"When we search for the ancient truths about architecture in the oldest historic layers, we consider not merely the remains left in the ground, but our language, the architerms, in order to understand what they have to say for the essence of habitation."

"The garden around the house is called 'life' in Hungarian. The walls of the house are plastered with earth, they are 'hidden'. The house has a foundation (in Hungarian 'leg') made of timber (in Hungarian 'foot', 'paws'). ..."

"Man entered through a gate to the enclosed piece of land called 'life'. The 'wings' of the gate opened, hanging on the so-called 'idols', 'keepers', 'guards' (the side timber of the frame). Even in the last century, and in some places in Transylvania until today, these 'idols' are carved from wood with magic inscriptions."

"The side timbers of the entrance door were called 'eagles' and above them were placed the upper beams of the frame

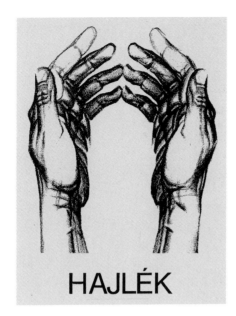

HAJLÉK

Hajlék, Catalog Cover, 1987, by György Csete. The shelter of the bough.

"Only from Pure Sources", Plate 25: The home of man as dug from the earth and shaped through interior transformations.

called 'eyebrows'. ... The windows-eyes which look at the 'life' are placed on the 'forehead' of the 'face' of the house. In the center of the house under the chimney was the fire and the place was defined from above by the central load-bearing beam which carried the tiebeams – 'mothers', supporting the ceiling. All this was held by a belt, 'crown' on which by means of 'elbows' or 'lips' are joined the rafters called 'horns'. The upper part of the 'horns' is joined to the 'backbone' – the ridge."

"The above description shows that our language still preserves the words of the ancient building traditions. Furthermore, building art itself uses not only this specific construction terminology, but points out to a particular view of life with a magic force which today seems a bit unusual and with a context lost deep in our consciousness. Today, when we say a 'backbone' or 'forehead' we do not feel in ourselves the expressive power of the words."

"Today these terms are used in the construction lexicon unintentionally. We use the term 'face' for the outside surfaces of the huge prefabricated blocks of flats. We call the numerous windows 'eyes'. But we do not possess the mental picture of such a 'face' behind which live thousands of people who observe the world through these openings. These huge houses have walls but do not have 'crests', nor 'backbones' for roofs. At the top of the wall something called a roof slab, grows a forest of aerials, of inside eyes, overgrown with the silent cluster of wires, with bizarre metal bushes. ... But only 50–60 years of this have passed in comparison to the several thousands of years of our 'roof' past."

"Here in Europe, houses always had roofs. The roofing – the 'forelock' of the roof was made of wood, tiles, pressed tiles, stone slabs, reed, straw and very rarely earth and grass. ... After the public death of international architecture, roofs have again returned to popularity. The steep roof is not only a better protection against rain, not only protects the walls from dampness, provides attics suitable for living and is much cheaper, but it is more beautiful. We all know it is cozy, the house is 'more of a house'."

The continuation of rural houses as cultural relics had been an essential part of the political program, since the communist takeover in 1948. Presumably the rural house represented the old standards against which the advantages of modern life could be compared. Open air folk museums are now found everywhere around the country, well-maintained, and well-furnished and sometimes with parts in operating order. Sometimes they are nationally sponsored, sometimes sponsored by the county or even the local municipality or village. The Göcsef Village Museum in Zalaegerszeg opened in 1968, the Open Air Museum at Szentendre founded in 1967 first opened in 1974.

By 1990 there were over 100 locally preserved indigenous buildings as examples of traditional types. The initiation of these activities in the late 1960s through the 1980s was parallel but independent of the rise of organic architecture. But deliberate ethnographic documentation and study was already well-established in the late 19th century with the political independence of Hungary.

But the continuity of indigenous construction has been an unconscious practice of many Hungarian architects throughout the twentieth century. The same architects who designed lifeless urban conglomerations in Budapest had another side. They were very comfortable with thatch roofs and mud or stone walls when designing for the countryside, whether the building was a traditional design or more adaptive. Because such construction is usually without a loan or mortgage, there are no outside controls. And because virtually all the construction materials are unprocessed they are both inexpensive and nontoxic and thus ecologically responsible. These practices deeply rooted in self-reliance and local wisdom are also fundamental to organic architecture.

By the mid 1980s the thatch roof was again becoming popular. Being associated with traditions and old-fashioned comfort it was especially used for highway restaurants and tourist shops. No sign or billboard was necessary, the building said hospitality. But during the 1950s and 1960s thatch was often forbidden on the basis of fire hazard, and rejected for its appearance of poverty. As late as the 1970s old thatch roofs in villages were removed or never replaced. However, a shift in social perceptions, as well as information about traditional fire treatment such as water glass and clay helped to change attitudes.

Indeed since the 1880s traditional rural architecture has inspired architects to develop a particularly national expression. One example among the memorable Hungarian vernacular images are the agricultural cellars set in a south-facing hillside at Cák in a western border valley southwest of Köszeg. Their simple rectangular early 19th century floor plans were originally intended to store chestnuts. They are now used for wine. Horizontal oak logs are plastered inside and outside with an adobe mixture of clay with straw or pig hair to keep out the wind and rain. With thatched gabled roofs they are classic examples of the appropriate uses of local materials.

For organic architects the conscious re-examination of traditional materials and construction methods as well as the imagery of cosy shelter have been deliberate vehicles of architectural renewal. Among the earliest, beginning in 1964, was a series of rural restaurants or highway road houses designed by Imre Makovecz working in the state planning office Szöyterv. Not very successful was the fish restaurant Haifisch at Valence. For

Agricultural Storehouses, at Cák, 18th and 19th century. Thatch roof, storage loft, oak log walls plastered with mud mixed with straw or pig hair and whitewashed.

Restaurant Sió Csárda, Szekszárd

Sió Csárda outside Szekszárd, 1964–1966, by Imre Makovecz.
Domestic imagery for a modern roadside tavern and restaurant.

Makovecz it was almost his first building. It was said of this particular state-owned restaurant that the owner had no sense of architecture, and the architect had no sense of restaurant. Its aggressiveness and open mouth immediately gave it the nickname "Capa", shark, as it continues to be known.

More successful was the Sió Csárda outside Szekszárd completed in 1966. It was for the same chain but at a smaller scale. Two connected thatched farmhouse shapes separate the tavern from the restaurant. With cellars below the raised terraces, the glass end walls allow outdoor use and a view over the parking lot into the countryside. Both scale and materials suit the intimate rural atmosphere of this design. For Makovecz, it was a personal shift from a modern and international architecture to a modern Hungarian architecture.

Probably the finest of these thatched yet modern regional inns by Imre Makovecz was the 1967 Csákanyosi Csárda at Tatabánya, destroyed by fire in 1979. In 1969 in one of the surprises of a heavily controlled political system, one of the architectural rebels received a national award. Makovecz was given the Ybl Prize, the highest honor for an architect. It was for new uses of traditional materials, especially for the set of restaurants that included Sió Csárda at Szekszárd.

Unlike conditions in the West, where the design of single-family houses continues as a kind of initiating experience for young architects, in Hungary as in other socialist countries, fresh graduates began professional work on big buildings in large state offices. In general, few single-family houses were built because that was outside the national social and economic plan. In Hungary it was possible to build a small private house in a provincial town or village where they could be overlooked. But these discrete buildings conformed to traditional plans and materials and would not be designed by architects. Thus, experience with single-family houses was not part of the creative culture of architecture until the beginning of the 1980s, when both the political and economic system began to shift. Even then, although architects could hardly either be allowed or afford their own practice, they could design privately after work hours.

The theme of the cozy peasant cottage, the traditional concept of shelter expressed in a new organic architecture, was first shown by the house constructed between 1978–1980 designed by András Erdei for László Péterfy, then a wood carver. Near a spring in the center of the village of Velem, it is in the very west of Hungary near Köszeg and near the Cák cellars. A double house scheme with two gable ends projecting out of the hillside it resembles the Sió Csárda. Workshops are below. A bold central ramp to a cantilevered balcony leads to a large major living hall and gallery and sleeping area. A large central hearth symbolizes the sun and focuses the assembly of wood carvers.

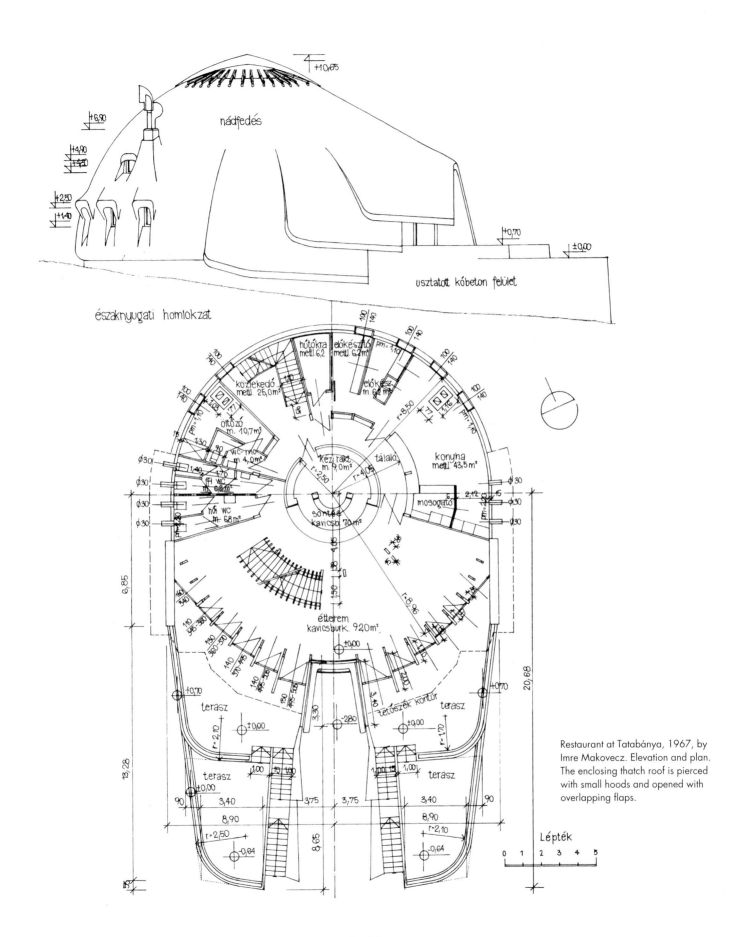

nádfedés

+10,65

+6,90

+4,90
+4,50

+2,50

+1,40

+0,70

±0,00

usztatott kőbeton felület

északnyugati homlokzat

hűtőkra mettl 6,2 előkészítő mettl 6,2 m²

pm=1,10

100 140

100 140

100 140

100 140

közlekedő mettl 25,0 m²

előkész. m. 6,2 m²

r=8,50

konyha mettl 43,5 m²

ø30

öltöző m. 10,7 m²

wc-mo m. 4,0 m²

kézi rakt. m. 9,0 m²

tálaló

r=2,50

r=4,05

mosogató

2,12

ø30

fH WC m. 6,2 m²

ø30

ø30

nöi WC m. 6,8 m²

söntés kavicsb. 70 m²

ø30

r=8,96

20,68

étterem
kavicsburk. 9,20 m²

+0,00

+0,70

6,85

tetőszék kontúr

+0,70

terasz

terasz

+0,00

+1,70

+0,00

terasz

+0,00

terasz

13,28

-2,80

3,30

1,00 15 1,00

1,00 15 1,00

90

3,40

3,75

3,75

3,40

90

8,90

8,90

8,65

r=2,50

-0,84

r=2,10

-0,64

Restaurant at Tatabánya, 1967, by
Imre Makovecz. Elevation and plan.
The enclosing thatch roof is pierced
with small hoods and opened with
overlapping flaps.

Lépték

0 1 2 3 4 5

Woodcarvers House, Velem

The architect András Erdei explained, "My designs are not creations of fantasy, or of production or economy, but creations of my ancestor life. They are part of a continuity, concerning housemaking, lovemaking, knowing each other. In a word: honor for life". Thus, the wood carver's house had an ambitious goal. Erdei had been asked in 1978 to organize a workshop for Péterfy's wood carver friends from Vas country. The house was intended to be a meeting place to encourage revival of the craft as an integrated part of contemporary life. In developing a continuing program, a series of other structures were also designed and constructed.

The first, a covered bridge built to replace an earlier one destroyed, became a symbolic gateway and link to the grounds. The dragon gate halfway between the bridge and the house intensifies the passage and the linkage. A number of other structures and a variety of wood carvings resulted from the ongoing

Woodcarvers House at Velem, 1978–1980, by András Erdei. A large lodge with workshops to encourage craft revival fits into the hillside with the appearance of two linked cottages.

series of workshops. Especially interesting in its use of materials was the wood storage shed and shop.

The house and the critical adjacent structures were completed by 1981 with the participation of 30 to 35 woodcarvers as part of a revitalization program for their craft. The social goals and the place of the architect were revealed in Erdei's comment from 1984 on the Velem experiment:

"There is room for doubt regarding the architectural method employed in the building of the workshop in Velem. I am sure that this is not the best solution to reinterpreting and humanizing architecture in our present time. It has its problems. But one thing is certain: Beyond the technical and architectural scope of the task I was pleased because a living community accepted me, and not only me, but a whole house that entailed a concept which I never dared to dream of before. Everybody suffers from the lack of a sense of community. What kinds of artificial forms do we create in lieu of examining the cause of this alienation? When we verged on losing this kinship suddenly a gate became ready, soon afterward a plan was made, and a few months later a house. I think we built a memorial to common work, belief, and thought. We became believers again, believers in Man."

The finest of the several Erdei structures for the Velem wood carvers may be the wood storage shed, 1979–1982. This elementary and naturally ventilated shelter using the traditional construction of lapped horizontal boards, and woven willow saplings is handsome and dignified without either sentimentality or story telling. Erdei's untimely death (1946–1986) left the organic movement without a dedicated communicator and articulate spokesman, conversant in several languages including Russian and English. As a mediator and peacemaker Erdei had arranged the first international exhibition of "A New Wave in Hungarian Architecture" in 1981 in Helsinki.

The conscious exploration of the shelter quality of hajlék was also initiated by György Csete independently after his return to Budapest from Pécs. The modest suburban three-story row house from 1978–1979, the three-unit Ujjady House in the Buda hills is a clean and quiet essay using a sheltering roof in red tile. It is in almost seamless continuity with anonymous and ubiquitous Hungarian roof forms.

But a major design statement by Csete is the artist's house initiated in 1979 near the top of the hill at Szentendre overlooking the folk museum far below. The Katai House is an animate body, a house deliberately sheltering diverse spirits. Deceptively simple in plan this building is sequentially ordered and spatially complex. The scheme is polarized by the dominance of two vertical cylindrical elements; one of glass located on the western perimeter, and one which is solid, located on the eastern interior.

Woodcarvers House at Velem. Ceremonial double doors at top of ramped stair lead into a social hall.

Woodcarvers House at Velem in the background, left is the Dragon Gate and right the wood storage shed with lapped boarding and woven willow sapling walls.

Katai House, Szentendre

Katai House at Szentendre, 1979–1986, by György Csete. The west end interprets the old image of house in traditional thatch roof and mud walls.

Katai House at Szentendre. The insulating thatch roof has small hooded openings aligned to sunrise on winter solstice, equinox, and summer equinox.

Katai House at Szentendre. The vertical greenhouse in the west wall serves as a lens to the outside world.

Approached from the street, the artist's house appears to be the "quintessential house" from Hungarian prememory. A sheltering oversized thatch roof generously protects a curved, textured, embracing whitewashed wall built of adobe. Three small circular window eyes bubble up through the thatch, evocative and mysterious in their intent.

The house is entered in the middle along the long south side, a traditional Hungarian arrangement. This contrasts with the formal classical bilateral symmetry of the house around the longitudinal axis. The first floor has a kitchen, living area, sunspace, and auxiliary spaces. Stairs curve upward around the curved east end to the second floor which has two bedrooms, a bathroom and an additional living/sunspace area. The two living areas on the west side are connected by a two-story interior open space that holds the vertically continuous sunspace.

The west-facing glass sunspace projects both outside and inside the house. Built of a number of small panes, this two-story, plant-filled crystaline cylinder is full of vegetative life, and is the primary source of light for the interior. It is similar to the multifaceted glass sphere on top of the Spring House at Orfü but in a new location and for new purposes. It is a symmetrical transparent crystal that links the cosmos with the interior, a bridge of green life linking between the outer and inner worlds.

On both floors, the west side spaces of the house are bright, outward focusing, and represent the spiritual aspects of daily living with light and air. The interior east cylinder contains a fireplace retreat on the ground level, and a bathroom on the second level. This area of the house is introspective and mortal, and concerned with the base elements of fire and water.

The eastern end of the building contains stairs, and must be walked through to get to the second level. This area, behind the fire and water is the most earthen area of the house. The ceiling is exposed bare thatch, 60 centimeters thick, and the odor of straw permeates the building. The area is dark, the only light entering this primitive nest-like womb is through the three small circular windows piercing the thatch. Rather than provide view, these openings are aligned to admit the first rays of the sun at winter solstice, equinox, and at the summer solstice. Moving from the east end of the house to the west, one must move from the dark to the light, closed to open, from body to spirit, an alternating experience that occurs constantly during the activities of daily living.

From the exterior, the west side of the building is open, it is the "face" of the structure. Its greenhouse "eye" admits sunlight and living substance, and its thatch "hair" shades its brow. The building appears as a proud temple from the west, humble from the east. The house is clearly referential to the textures and forms of the traditional Hungarian "folk" house, and thus responds to the reality of material culture with its heavy adobe walls and trimmed thick thatch. But as solar architecture, the Katai house while thermally sound in the heat lag and thermal storage of its mud brick walls, is mostly symbolic in its link to the cosmos.

The use of local materials, not for sentimental or ecological reasons but for practical expedience is well represented by the rammed earth walls, similar to adobe construction in the Csaladi house at Zalaszentgrót, a small town of 12,000 in western Hungary. Designed by Tibor Jankovics, it was completed in 1985 for an entrepreneurial truck driver who now runs a chicken farm.

This is the architect's first building using earth materials. Although the use of sun-dried brick and of rammed earth is traditional in Hungary, it is invisible since it is always covered with a heavy stucco and then painted. So it is impossible to estimate how many of the older buildings are of unbaked earthen construction. For this house no add-mixtures such as asphalt were used. With only seven months of construction time this house was completed very quickly and thus required extensive drying out after occupation.

The design is a classic and symmetrical rectangular cottage. The middle third of the bilateral plan is centered by a large oven fireplace inspired by traditional designs and backed by a stair to the upper loft. Facing the small garden and covered porches are kitchen and dining. On the other side of the fireplace is the living room separated from the street by an entry porch and winter garden with a large glazed south-facing bay. These social spaces provide differentiated functions within a large space dominated by the fireplace, a strong statement of family and shelter. They are flanked on both sides by bedrooms and bathrooms. The central fireplace has a special meaning in Hungary since historically this was the focus of every peasant house. The fire was tended continuously. And since at one stage there was a chimney tax there is also the tradition of avoiding chimneys but allowing the smoke to penetrate the attic keeping rodents under control and preserving homemade sausages. "Under one smoky fire you can arrange everything", is a Hungarian saying.

The roofing of brown beaver tail clay tile looks like wood shingles. But the special character of the sheltering organic roof comes from the swelling form in the center and from the slight curve at the eave line all around the roof edge. Similarly the heavy white walls have sharp corners but bulge out slightly in plan expressing the life of their handmade construction.

By 1984, of the 70,000 new housing units built in Hungary annually, between 30,000 and 32,000 were built by farmers and villagers for their own use. Typically they were completed without mortgages and were constructed with the help of relatives and friends. This sweat equity by simple builders using

Katai House at Szentendre. A traditional Hungarian beehive stove is in the center of the plastered adobe interior.

Csaladi House, Zalaszentgrót

Csaladi House at Zalaszentgrót, 1984–1985, by Tibor Jankovics. Built of heavy traditional materials, the exterior appears conservative and closed, but with subtle shifts of plane and edge.

Csaladi House at Zalaszentgrót. A traditional fireplace and loft under the high part of the roof is central to an open kitchen, dining, living space.

local materials did not encourage innovation. Typically traditional or stock plans were used.

However, limited privatization by the mid 1980s brought architectural opportunities. Custom houses in the Buda hills suburbs of Budapest again became an opportunity for architectural exploration and statement as it had been before World War II. It also became a critical part of Makovecz's architectural development and his viability as an independent architect. Within his relatively large production of custom house designs common themes reoccur. At first, Makovecz tried not to copy himself and relished each new creative opportunity. But "after the 15th house that attempts to be creative by going back to basics, the results may not be so unique". Inevitably certain patterns of logic and insight persisted and became repeated.

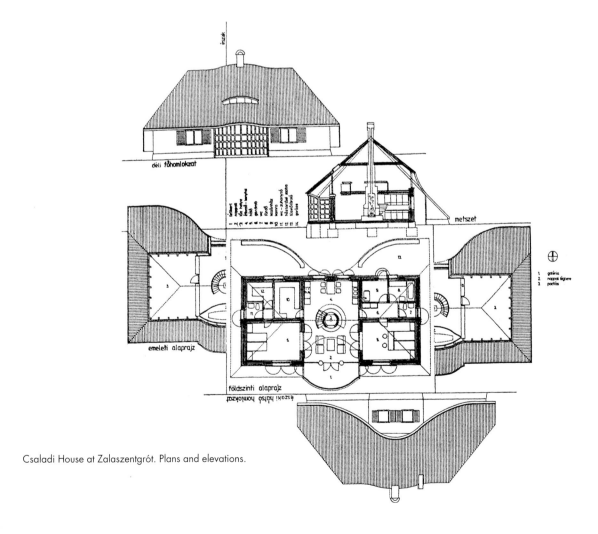

Csaladi House at Zalaszentgrót. Plans and elevations.

The double house at 25 Törökvészi designed in 1983 and completed in 1986 was the first of several houses with plans of interlocking circles by Makovecz. Built for Lajos Gubsci, a high-ranking Party member, the house sits high on the crest of a hill surrounded by a wall and guard dogs. The circles make a series of interior pavilions with exposed wood ceilings and free-standing tree columns. Some have suggested the circular plan is inspired by the design of yurts. But here the scale and the complexity of overlapping conically topped cylinders is much more kaleidoscopic. Especially on the upper floor the effect of deeply protected wood caverns is heightened by the cone-shaped roofs capped by a skylight. The expansive exterior galleries have magnificent views to the south. Another set of balconies faces west. The circular clustering suggests both a protective multiple encampment as well as a generous rustic lookout.

Gubsci House, Budapest

Gubsci House at Budapest, 1983–1986, by Imre Makovecz. A protective encampment of interlocked open and closed pavilions overlooks the Buda Hills.

Gubsci House at Budapest. Wood stairs with open risers step up into the tree-columned shelter.

Gubsci House at Budapest. Soaring space within the intersection of domed and cone-roofed pavilions.

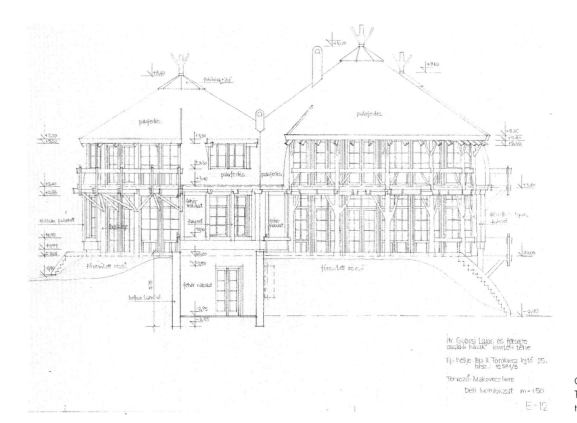

Gubsci House at Budapest. South elevation. The facade is almost totally glazed behind the porches.

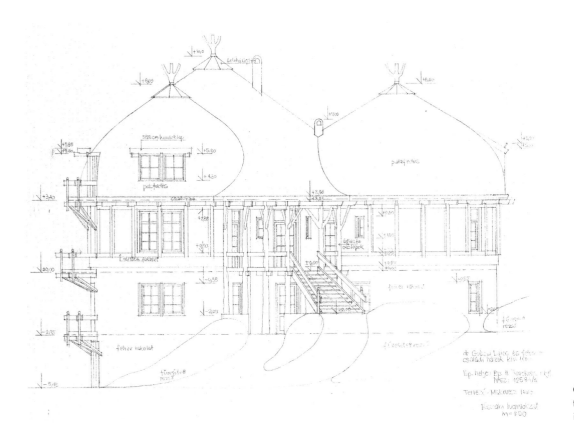

Gubsci House at Budapest. Pencil construction drawing of east elevation showing three intersecting circular pavilions.

Pete and Megyeri House, Budapest

Another double house but a duplex for two entrepreneurial owners was in a suburban valley at 9 Kondorkert. Owner Ernö Pete did his own interior finish woodwork, while Lajos Megyeri used a professional carpenter, and then sold his unit. Thus, there are some variations in detail between the sides. Set back in a spacious lawn the double L-shaped design suggests middle-class privacy and security. The side-by-side but separate walks and stairs up the middle lead to distinct entrances in the recessed central terrace. Garages provide a visual base for the raised and protected terrace in front of the main floor. Monumental chimneys in the center of each dwelling also have a structural role. Upstairs bedrooms are sheltered inside red-tiled naves like upside-down boats. Orientation to the southwest allows the well-protected full windows to get generous winter sun. Glass doors allow the living space to flow outside to the terrace. With wall construction of hollow clay terracotta tile and timber roofs that again use tree columns, it is a construction using familiar materials.

Pete and Megyeri House at Budapest, 1983–1986, by Imre Makovecz. Raised on a common service platform, the hooded tile roofs open to the south, expressing the two households.

Pete and Megyeri House at Budapest. Tree column branches support the balcony framing.

Pete and Megyeri House at Budapest. The tiled roof lifts to protect the two entrances.

110

Houses in more rural settings offered different constraints. On the bank of the Danube 25 kilometers upriver from Budapest at Göd, Makovecz designed a bold house in 1986 for his old school classmate Ödön and his wife Katalin Dóczy, both veterinarians. Completed in 1988 the roof and walls make a continuous single rounded wooden shape. Like a rock nestled in the mature trees, its softended forms and natural textures quickly disappear in nature. Although superficially similar to the wood shingled ski lift at Dobogókö, this is a multi-story private house where the single rustic enclosure provides discrete and spacious privacy with a view. The carport and entrance are absorbed within the wood shell. On the interior there is a partial balcony to the raised main floor as well as a partial floor at the lower ground level. With a twisted floor plan and the soaring lines of roof rafters and braces, the space ultimately focuses on the view. Only on the west does the shell discretely open with a large protected and cantilevered balcony to expose the great curving expanse of the Danube flowing in the sunset. Windows seem to disappear.

A retirement house with a different set of ideas about building in nature is the villa on Mecsek Mountain overlooking Pécs designed by Sándor Dévényi. Completed in 1988 it is a house of several dimensions, appropriate to its mountain side setting. The eastside, walled with fieldstone is closed and holds the nighttime and sleeping spaces. Windows are hidden under the eaves. The westside is arched and framed with a stucco wall and many windows to contain the day spaces. A protected central glazed entrance opens into a spacious stone-lined hall with stairs rising to the upper story as cut stone terraces without handrails. Simultaneously the symmetrical boarded ceiling with its exposed dark structural ribs moves upwards. The bipart theme continues with two separate apartments, one for a male, the other a female. Private outdoor terraces extend the distinct living spaces. These contrasting ideas of spaces and materials are folded into an architectural continuity that assures privacy between the parts, yet harmony of the whole.

Dóczy House, Göd

Dóczy House at Göd, 1986–1988, by Imre Makovecz. The continuous enclosure of broad board shingles is opened only by a balcony cantilevered toward the Danube.

Dóczy House at Göd. Carport and entrance are discretely absorbed within the wood boarded form.

Left: Villa on Mecsek Mountain at Pécs, 1986–1988, by Sándor Dévényi.

Villa on Mecsek Mountain at Pécs. Cut stone stairs and platform without handrails provide central circulation hall and neutral zone between separate apartments.

Weisz House, Mohács

More modest are the houses designed by István Kistelegdi in Pécs and smaller towns in southwestern Hungary. The Weisz House in Mohács, completed 1987, is typical as a creative variant on the characteristic town or village house. Traditional construction is stucco-covered brick walls and timber-trussed red-tile roofs. In such custom houses special design attention is extended to the doors and windows. The side to the street is relatively anonymous and is built right up to the building line. But an L-shaped plan opens the compact two-story scheme to the side and rear yard. Economical of land, the house – partly facing south – interacts with terrace, garden, and fruit trees. On the interior a circular stair rising in a central stair hall crowned by a pyramidal skylight emphasizes the vertical axis. As is typical in the Hungarian villages the main entry is on the side and is controlled by a gate along the street.

More dynamic is the Végvári House at Miskolc by Ferenc Salamin of the new generation of organic architects. Like the traditional Hungarian village house, its end faces the street. But the traditional monolithic form shifts at midpoint, and the sheltering roof and stepped sidewalls have been set into lively motion. Two porches slide under the roofs. Traditionally compartmented rooms open into each other providing new spatial juxtapositions while retaining solid repose. The old is rejuvenated.

Weisz House at Mohács, 1987, by István Kistelegdi. The traditional lineal Hungarian house plan with its porch is turned 90 degrees to embrace a compact suburban garden.

Végvári House, Miskolc

Végvári House at Miskolc, 1989–1993, by Ferenc Salamin of Axis. The traditional compact house form is enlivened by the rolling roof surfaces, bold-shaped openings, and a midpoint shift in massing.

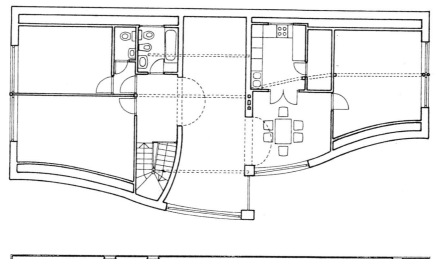

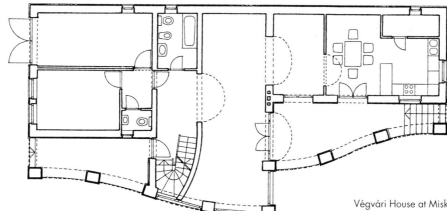

Végvári House at Miskolc. The first and ground floor (below) plans reveal two central living halls, creating a variety of distinct but interlocked spaces for two households. Two side porches provide traditional protected outdoor space.

Végvári House at Miskolc. The curve of windows continues the form of the roof.

Tibor Jakob House, Solymár

In Solymár, a village northwest of Budapest, at 23 Bocskai is the two-story Tibor Jakob House. Designed by Imre Makovecz in 1988 it was completed in 1991 for the family of a school teacher. Like the traditional Hungarian village house the gable end of the red-tiled roof faces the street and the daily entrance is in the middle of the long side. However here a formal door and stairs also faces the street on the end, symmetrically protected by an open porch. The kitchen is in the center of the house with the living and dining spaces downstairs facing the large rear garden. The master bedroom on the balcony above overlooks the living area. The garden end of the house is rounded, fully glazed and open to the south. A single large white masonry column structurally supports the radiating roof purlins and centers the two-story family space.

This circular temple form on its raised stone terrace with its generous roof supported by tree columns is a pure statement of prototypical prememory architecture. Its powerful clarity is enlivened by the play of peeled tree trunks and branches reaching upward to support the cone of the roof. Its elementary geometry provides a strong image of shelter.

Tibor Jakob House at Solymár, 1988–1991, by Imre Makovecz. The main facade is aligned like the traditional house with the gable end to the street.

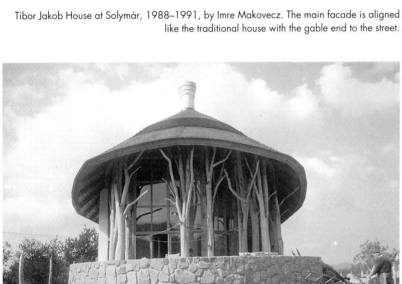

Tibor Jakob House at Solymár. The garden end of the house is a raised pavilion under a conical roof.

Urban Housing

Organic Interventions

Urban life is distinguished by the architectural patterns of city dwelling. In Europe a traditional prototype is the multi-story and multi-use apartment block. This is a pattern that emerged from the medieval row house where artisan work space or warehouse or shop occupied the accessible ground floor, and family living space occupied upper floors. In the increased urban density of the 19th century this pattern typically emerged as a series of blocks on the street line with shops at the ground level, and apartments above. Since they were walk-up buildings they were between three and five stories high. The use of courtyards provided access to light and air. Identifiable entrances limited the number of apartments or flats off each stairway. In central Europe such an interactive architectural idea of urban life often associated with coffee-house culture has many variations.

Even in a small country like Hungary a surprising heterogeneity of urban housing block designs existed within a city, as well as between cities. Both in the provincial centers and the heavily populated capital, Budapest, there was great diversity of design within this standard prototype. Central European practice also encouraged broad mixes within the same block. The large spacious apartments and suites for the middle class faced out over the tree-lined boulevards. But in the other three sides of these large blocks could be one-room ordinary flats for the poor and the working class overlooking tight inner courtyards. The diversity of eclectic architectural details especially from the urbanization of the late 19th century, the "belle epoque", added to the charm of individual blocks, to the distinction of each neighborhood, as well as to the unique character of each city.

But the wounds to the historical continuity of this urban fabric as a result of World War II and the following political regimes have lasted half a century. In 1991 Ákos Moravánszky wrote about Budapest:

"Where else in the world can a person find so much lead and exhaust in the air, so much crumbling plaster, so many dirty synthetic materials, such crowded streets, as in this Central European metropolis? Yet, the texture of the past is still to be most easily discovered in the vacant lots, between the fire walls; here, the rips in the fabric of history emerged. In those places where a fissure severs the smooth surface, the layers in the shaft of excavation are visible. In an extraordinary way, the bizarre kiosks, the old neon lights, the noise and the use of elbows in the underpasses continually reload the residents with energy. This exchange occurs via the high degree of tension which, in the end, results in the atmosphere of these cities. This atmosphere can be felt in Budapest at Moszkva Square or in the district around the Otthon department store ... Today, Eastern Central Europe is run down and vulgar ..."

This urban neglect was in part a result of the national housing policies throughout Europe both East and West after World War II. The goal was to produce necessary housing as quickly as possible. Everywhere this was achieved by mass production high-rise housing at the periphery of major cities – whole new quarters based on perversions of Le Corbusier's prewar idealism of the "radiant city" with large apartment blocks standing freely in a sunlit park while ignoring the inner city. Shopping and other daily needs were separated from housing.

In Hungary the architecture of Soviet Social Realism with its neoclassicism that replaced the avant-garde of constructivism had little effect. But with the death of Stalin in 1953 it was the post-Stalin policies of the Soviet Union that dominated. At the Moscow Party congress of 1954 when Kruschev denounced the "unnecessary ornament" and "empty formalism" of Social Realism, he replaced it with a mass-production simplified variant of the International Style. As elsewhere, architects in Hungary worked in large government-run design offices under the Ministry of Construction Industry that were organized like a manu-

Old and new housing, Obudai Street at Budapest. Like elsewhere in Europe, postwar industrialized housing produced violent contrasts with older urban environments.

Hillside Terrace Houses at Pécs, 1977, by Csaba, Dévényi and Weiler. Stepped multi-family housing on the southern slopes of Mecsek Mountain.

Rákóczi Street Apartments, Pécs

Rákóczi Street Apartments at Pécs, 1984, by István Kistelegdi. The rear facade overlooks the old City Wall with glazed cantilevered corridors as apartment access.

facturing industry. The uniform monotony of industrialized construction produced a drab and anonymous built environment that ultimately infused alienation and destroyed community.

The frustrating soullessness of these endless apartment blocks challenged architects. But especially the new generation such as Makovecz who had witnessed the Russian suppression of the 1956 revolution also realized that while prefabricated housing provided accommodation it simultaneously regulated lives in totally mechanical patterns. All had the same small balcony. All buildings had the same orientation. It had nothing to do with the sun and rarely had any relationship to site. Every individual apartment had the same plan. The family size was the same. The TV sat only in one place. Every evening throughout the country people sat facing in the same position – the television viewing was polarized by the architecture of room layout and land planning. They were reductionist buildings with a minimalist mentality: easy to build and easy to operate. Simultaneously, they provided social isolation and acoustic amplification. On the third floor you could hear a family quarrel on the first floor.

There were almost no opportunities for architects to respond creatively. Primarily it was only in historic renovation and restoration of select locations, and on awkward shaped land plots that interesting or attractive new housing designs were possible. But this had to wait for the 1980s to happen in a few sites in a few cities remote from Budapest: in places where there were needs for custom-designed infill housing projects, and where local authorities were sensitive to the possibilities. Here both the ethical standards and the creative aesthetic of the young organic architects responded to select opportunities. In Pécs a playful series of identical hillside dwellings at 8 Kalinin was completed already in 1977 by a team composed of Gyula Csaba, Sándor Dévényi, and Árpád Weiler. As ten freehold houses among the terraced gardens and vineyards they stepped up the south-facing slope of Mecsek Mountain. Each had full solar access plus a patio and view over the city. Most distinctive were the curved profiles of the firewalls that provided scale in bold ripples along the hill. Garages facing the street provided privacy and a base for the development. The complex was bisected by an internal pedestrian street dancing up the mountain under a serpentine canopy of curved pipe and translucent plastic.

The large apartment block also in Pécs, at 35–37 Rákóczi demonstrated a more urban organic design. Designed by István Kistelegdi in 1984, it was completed in 1986. A major building on a major street near the center of a large historic city, it conforms to the pattern of the European housing block. At ground level shops open directly off the sidewalks. Facing south, the street elevation has four different bands of window

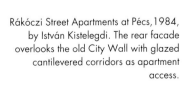

Rákóczi Street Apartments at Pécs.
Window composition was stimulated by the
availability of a single square glass size.

treatment primarily developed using square panes. Especially the fan-shaped wrought iron balcony rails display a certain elegance in refinement. The hooded roof with generous dormer projections continues the sheltering theme of roof. This design confidence is continued on the north side facing the old city wall where access balconies are screened by reeded glass walls set in a wave pattern. Access to the apartment floors is through a lobby of curved walls with stairs that spiral up. A column in the center of the lobby supports a roof dome, capped with a skylight oculus.

Rákóczi Street Apartments at Pécs. The shops at sidewalk level are clearly differentiated from the stacked apartments above. The architecture respects the line of buildings along the street while inflecting its own entrance.

Rákóczi Street Apartments at Pécs. Street elevation.

Kistelegdi's organic design skill in this urbane block in Pécs has been continued in smaller projects as well as several commercial complexes that are also woven into the old fabric of Pécs. At 41 Anna in Pécs and a block south of the 13th and 14th century city wall, a four-family row house infill was completed in 1985. It is a traditional Pécs scheme with a central arched gate to the rear garden. However, the site was difficult because of underground water and a steep irregular site. The four garages along the street became a retaining wall. Thus, each dwelling has a front door facing the rear garden on the second level. The orderly street facade is a bold composition of restudied and contrasting traditional elements. The four dormers with their generous gable surrounds provide picturesque and lively silhouettes above the cornice line.

Anna Street Apartments, Pécs

Anna Street Apartment House at Pécs, 1985, by István Kistelegdi. The street facade of this infill housing maintains the cornice line and the rhythm of windows and dormers of the existing buildings.

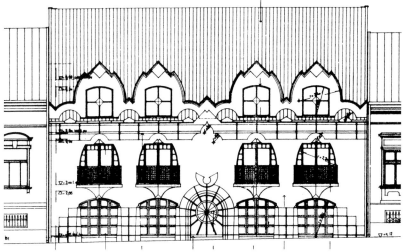

Anna Street Apartment House at Pécs. Elevation. At street level four garage doors and a gate.

Anna Street Apartment House at Pécs. Contrasting textures enhance the architectural details on a flat wall.

The Blasted Block at Pécs, 1978–1985, by Sándor Dévényi. Infill housing continues the historic line of buildings, cornice line, window rhythms, and even quoin geometry.

Blasted Block, Pécs

Also completed in 1985 in Pécs was the apartment addition designed in 1978 by Sándor Dévényi known either as "The House Struck by Lightning" or "The Blasted Block". The new wing faces the old mill street at 2 Felsömalom. The original building, the "Crown of Hungary", was a restaurant and hotel built shortly after 1792 when the city wall and moat were removed and the land was subdivided. The original two-story inn faced Kossuth Street, the major road to the east. Into this 200-year-old town palace a two story extension is matched to maintain street definition, cornice lines, and architectural rhythms. But a deliberate dialogue is designed between historical thesis and contemporary antithesis. The effect of continuity is achieved across this whimsical intellectual polarity, by substituting void where there should be solid, and negative where there should be positive. The recess joints between the rectangular stones of the old walls are continued in the new part as a grid screen of steel tubing. Window and door rhythms are duplicated as masonry frames but stand in isolation, unattached to solid walls; and the masonry spandrels of a balcony rail are repeated as panels of metal louvres.

The rift between old and new is a jagged fissure that accounts for the local description as "struck by lightning". But that detail and the charged architectural play between old and new are hardly noticeable against the strong calm of a well-proportioned facade. The character of the original one-story wing is maintained by the loggia on the new second story. A deep upper porch and a recessed wall behind the screen on the street at ground level provide private circulation and keep apartments back from the street. The rhythms of the upper colonnade and the strong shadow of the tiled roof make a statement of generous shelter. The former Baroque arched carriageway to the courtyard was suggested by the new thin steel overlaid arch that identifies the entrance into the new wing.

The rear faces an inner garden. Its wall is more straightforward; with continuous glass at the ground floor, and the same deep recessed balcony on the upper floor. With eight apartments, six chimneys, a garage below and new small shops it is a mixed-use scheme. But the whole building is expressed as a single unit from the street. A popular design it received the 1986 Hungarian Building of the Year Award.

This clever tongue-in-cheek building is even more striking since the architect is strongly identified with the "organic" movement where designs typically relied heavily on folk culture, and on free uses of traditional building materials. Sándor Dévényi as an architect was not part of the Pécs Group that broadened the local cultural content by initiating a new native architecture. Here there is no evidence of "organic forms" in Dévényi's designs. Only the method of thinking, the creative process, is organic. But the architectural forms are neoclassical. Dévényi's skill with eclectic Renaissance forms is rare in Hungary and especially is found nowhere else among the strongly organic designs of the new generation of architects.

Dévényi's professional education at the Technical University emphasized architectural history. He believes that only by appreciating the past can you understand your own work as a line of continuity. He especially sees the city of Pécs as a cultural window where ancient Hungarians looked to the west. The 2,000 years of history have included involvement with the Romans, Turks, Germans, and Slavs as well as the seat of the oldest university in Hungary.

But for Dévényi responding and enriching the historical setting is only one strategy. Another is to deliberately create new value. Especially in an urban context new designs must also initiate fresh settings. Dramatic, even brute freshness characterizes

The Blasted Block at Pécs. A jagged rift separates the historic 18th century fabric from the 20th century building.

his design of the Bull Head Block on an otherwise undistinguished street in Pécs' historical district.

Designed in 1982 and completed in 1989, the Bull Head Block at 3 Kazinczy at the corner of Perczel Street, gets its name from the bold attic feature that marks the intersection of the two streets. Characteristically the ground level contains shops and pulls pedestrians into the colonnade behind its heavy freestanding piers. That rectangular stepping geometry changes with the swelling curves of large bay windows on the next floor. Delicate filigree fans of ironwork and multiple projecting arches emphasize the generous but well-protected living spaces behind. The continuous band of openable windows under the horizontal eaves underlines the roof cornice. And within the sloped red-tile roofing, fanlight attic dormer windows continue the usable living space beyond the grand glazed and domed corner.

This rich yet orderly architectural diversity is reinforced by the structural logic. The bay windows are centered above the ground floor piers so that structural forces must be brought diagonally to the top of the piers. Even the color makes a clear separation between the private residential upper stories with their white walls, and the darker color and recessed shadow of public space at ground level.

A similar boldness of invention marks the 1988 Dévényi design of a private home. The "House that Eats Flats" or "Biting House" sits as a corner gateway at the bottom of a hill of middle class one-family houses in Málom that was once a separate village. It faces a large open development of prefabricated high-rise apartment blocks in South Pécs. This aggressive design is animated but not biomorphic. It functions as an urban landmark that celebrates the clash between two housing cultures.

Bull Head Block at Pécs, 1982–1989, by Sándor Dévényi. The shops are recessed deep behind a colonnade at street level. The apartments above have a contrasting expression.

Bull Head Block at Pécs. The wrought iron balustrade implies the generous apartment beyond.

"Biting House" at Málom near Pécs, 1988, by Sándor Dévényi.

As a collaborator in the 1985–1987 master planning of Paks under the leadership of Imre Makovecz, Sándor Dénényi was commissioned in 1987 to design a block of 32 flats for pensioners. Located next to the old Calvinist Church and completed in 1991 the block brought a new scale to the older section of this growing town inspired by the symmetrical quiet of country houses of nobility in 19th century Hungary. Taking advantage of the slope of the site a series of shops is located at the ground level with a pedestrian plaza. They were sold at high prices to help to finance the whole project. Architecturally, this gave the apartments on the upper two floors both privacy and security as well as separate entrances. By clustering and detailing the windows the building achieves a certain heroic grandeur and civic character overlooking a small park to the south with trees and a war memorial.

Pensioners Apartments, Paks

Pensioners' Apartments at Paks, 1987–1991, by Sándor Dévényi. The apartments are above a base of small shops.

Pensioners' Apartments at Paks. Civic scale is achieved by the repetition of a strongly articulated bay with a straight foundation and flat wall.

At Debrecen, the old city in the Great Hungarian Plain, a long-standing civic pride and a well-developed low-scale urban housing pattern demanded a different discipline. Although a city of essentially one-family houses of one and two stories, the effect of continuity along the street line is reinforced by the subtle architectural detailing of both the facades and gates that open into side and rear yards. Architect Attila Köszeghy, also the author of a publication on this centuries-old tradition, has gained a unique local reputation for deliberately exploring new expressions of public facades and gates, both by introducing visual movement as well as strong color and texture contrasts while maintaining the enclosure of the street plane.

Already his 1985 design for Zoltán Nagy at 58 Homok Street is plastic in the forms of its components. Further emphasis by using bold colors has not been completed. But the contrasting of a dark dormer to a white one, the reinforcement of the projecting three-sided bay window with sculptural stucco work, and the front door portico pulling out of the facade with one free column are seen as daring enrichments in this quiet Calvinist city on the plains.

Even more sweeping sculptural forms liberate Attila Készeghy's 1986 design for the Eisler House at 101 Apafi Street. As in the design on Homok Street the flatness of the street plane is maintained while the facade is put into motion. Similarly the interiors are designed to emphasize spatial flow with L-shaped rooms, the placement of windows, and the fluid sculpting of surfaces, especially ceilings.

In contrast is the perfectly flat facade of the Kiss House at 5 Faraktár in Debrecen by Imre Makovecz. Here careful proportions, finesse in detail, and exceptional craftsmanship bring fresh elegance to an essentially traditional composition of gate and window as the expressive events on the street wall.

In another city Makovecz conceived perhaps the most ambitious urban housing of the 1980s. In the center of Sárospatak the full city block that already contained his 1969 Bodrog Department Store (described in the following chapter), was master planned by Makona for a series of apartment buildings with shops and public spaces at ground level. Each building was then designed in a different studio of the Makona co-operative. Makovecz had initiated this project on Rákóczi Street as early as 1976. But it was 1982–83 until the first building was begun. Rectangular blocks with white walls and red-tile roofs with circular vaults and fan windows on the top floor gave the principle articulation. Arched openings at ground level provided access to shops.

The most interesting housing block in the Sárospatak plaza complex is the Pharmacy House Apartment named after its drug store and chemist shop at ground level beside the arched opening through the block. Designed by Ervin Nagy in 1983 and completed in 1985, the building is a cluster of bearing wall towers with hooded red-tile roofs facing south. The serrated plan forms and roof profiles are continued in the pattern of the arch-topped windows that bend around the corners of the towers. Picturesque variety is achieved with the repetition of a few characterful parts. But perhaps the sculpted balconies and terraces on the sides provide more spatial amenity as well as a better articulated elevation for urban housing. Set deep in the plaza the arched penetration of the block also provides a focus and a pedestrian link to buildings and schools to the north.

Apartment Buildings and Shops, Sárospatak

Rácóczi Street Apartments at Sárospatak, 1976–1982, by Imre Makovecz and Makona. Pedestrian precinct defined by walk-up housing with shops at ground level. The first building to be completed in 1982 by Makovecz, on the left. The last completed are the Pharmacy House Apartments by Nagy in the background.

Pharmacy House Apartment at Sárospatak,
1983–1986, by Ervin Nagy of Makona.
A serrated plan, wrap-around cut-out windows, and hooded windows breaking
through a red tile roof are the characteristic
features of the development.

Right: Rácóczi Street Apartments at Sárospatak.
Hooded stacks of balconies and bay
windows break through the white masonry
blocks at the corners.

Pharmacy House Apartment at Sárospatak.
The terraces and balconies are protected by
screen walls.

Rácóczi Street Apartments at Sárospatak. The early block masterplan by Makovecz with the final buildings.

Apartment Buildings, Gyongyös

In Gyongyös, a town of 20,000 people, there are two characterful multi-family buildings for electric power plant personnel. The evolution of the design program at Gyongyös illustrates the organic process of solution-seeking. The client, the electricity utility, needed apartment units and bought three adjacent old houses to be demolished to provide a large enough site. Otherwise the client had no special interests and expected a single building as a stack of flats, similar to other redevelopment in the neighborhood.

But the architects attempted to address larger issues of the community. The three sites were on a narrow residential street once of one-story houses. Already there was a new bulky three-story apartment building on one end. In addition it was a very large and deep block with one continuously built edge facing the

127

Apartment Buildings at Gyöngyös, 1987–1990, by László Vincze, Tibor Szalai, and Ferenc Salamin of Axis Studio. The garden side of the red-tiled design is deliberately in contrast with the yellow apartment building, designed simultaneously by the same studio.

Apartment Buildings at Gyöngyös. The access to the car parking in the basement is from the south-facing garden side of both buildings.

main street and many interior buildings. Therefore, a master plan was proposed for the whole block that included an interior road system and thus the potential of more infill building sites and a more dense development. Within this conceptual framework the Axis studio retained the boundary lines of the three existing houses. Each new building was designed as a separate project by a separate designer; as though there were different clients or the construction had been at different times. The studio made its own more demanding rules of how this new construction could contribute to the quality of the town.

The building at 10 Dozsa has a symmetrical yellow stucco three-story facade with roof dormers. It was designed in 1986 by László Vincze of the Axis Studio of Makona and completed in 1990. Two superscaled superimposed flat arches frame the central entry directly on the flat street facade. Two recessed

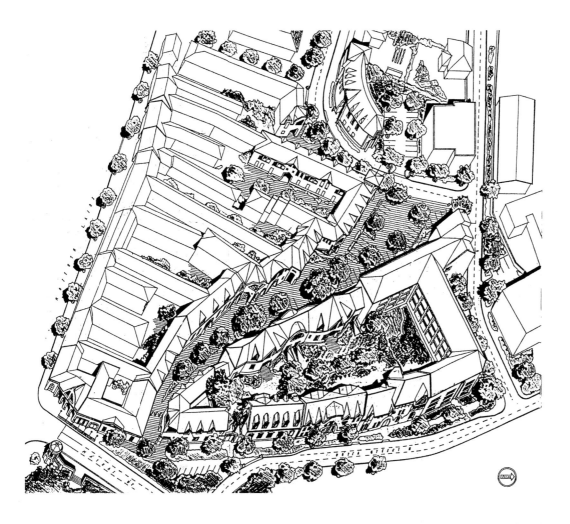

Apartment Buildings at Gyöngyös. Masterplan, showing more intensive development of the whole block including new internal circulation as a context for design of the three distinctive buildings at the bottom.

Apartment Buildings at Gyöngyös. The three apartment houses along Dozsa Street, on the right by Ferenc Salamin and center by László Vincze; the design on the left by Tibor Szalai remains a project.

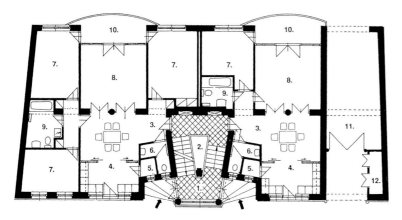

Apartment Buildings at Gyöngyös. Ground floor plan (Vincze). Bearing wall is around perimeter and down the center. The apartments have balconies and their largest windows on the south-facing garden side. On the right (11) drive-through and gate from street.

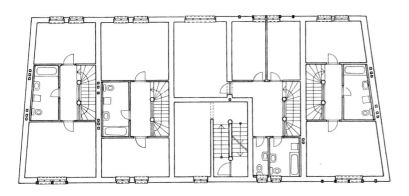

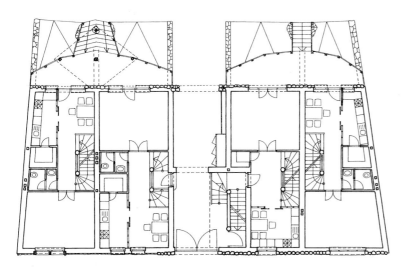

Apartment Buildings at Gyöngyös. First and ground floor plans (Salamin). The two-storey maisonnettes have direct access from outside; the living rooms alternately face the street or the garden side. The central passage and stairs lead to the attic flat.

entry doors provide the only depth along the narrow sidewalk. More modest scale and more interesting modeling is achieved in the rear elevation where six garages form a base for three stacks of apartments with their south-facing balconies crowned by hooded roofs. Back to back bath rooms provide plumbing economy and allow the clustering of all the flues from the individual gas fired furnaces.

The house next door, another multi-family residence, has fieldstone veneer and white walls, with steeply pitched red-tile roofs. Designed by Ferenc Salamin of Axis in 1986, it too was completed in 1989. Its asymmetrical liveliness with rustic stone work, dark-stained woodwork, exposed bracing, and deep balconies is much more articulated and also less urban. There are five apartments. Four are two-story units with an interior stair and reversed plans so that living rooms alternatively face the street or the rear yard. The fifth apartment is in the attic with dormer windows. A third design was not built because the existing house was occupied by a family that had some property claim of ownership prior to the communist period – a political issue that began to be addressed at the end of the 1980s.

A number of other recent apartment buildings continue the theme of how organic urban dwellings can add to richness and liveliness of the fabric of cities. Simultaneously they provide variety to the choices of accommodation. But these colorful and articulate designs have been built in such small numbers that they have made a minimal quantitative impact on housing. Nevertheless their demonstration of individuality and creativity within a standardized urban building prototype are models of organic urbanity.

130

Shopping and Commerce
Spaces for Business and Leisure

Outside Hungary organic architecture is conceived and practiced primarily as a rural or a suburban idea. Especially as a convincing commitment to design in and of nature, organic architecture has typically needed natural settings as well as natural materials. Particularly in the West where organic architecture is associated with the unique integrity of the individual and the singular integrity of a masterful design, realization has been as a series of distinctive and independent works in isolated settings.

In Hungary the concept of living architecture originated in the belief of an alive society, as well as in the team participations implicit in the Pécs Group and in the Makona co-operative. If organic architecture emerged as a Hungarian reaction to the environment built during the Russian occupation, as a subversive and artistic expression of political resistance, it also emerged as a collective act. Its concern with cultural identity was a group activity. Thus, organic architecture in Hungary demonstrated social responsibility at many levels. Most impressively, it was a participative process at an urban scale, but with the new inventive architecture.

Aside from urban housing, another level of engagement was concern with historic preservation. Contemporary needs in urban renewal required both the continuation of old urban prototypes and the invention of new ones, including shops, plazas, and mixed uses of public and semi-private spaces. Organic designs attempted to become living developments with significant cultural content, not just restyled commercial or commemorative structures. Even less visible was the re-establishment and expansion of cultural identity through an organic form of urban renewal. The subtle seamless reweaving of Kecskemét over 20 years by József Kerényi into a new identity, and the more visible transformations of Pécs were parallel and successful stories of different needs and solutions.

In spite of its long-standing cultural traditions, Hungary has a recent political identity. Architectural expression of the modern nation did not flower until later in the 19th century. Within a generation of the union of Pest, Buda and Óbuda in 1873, Budapest became one of the finest and most important cities of Europe. Simultaneously the enthusiastic emergence of several local styles of architecture by the turn of the century provided richly detailed, heterogeneous and often eclectic expressions for public as well as private spaces. Thus, there was the Historicism of the conservatives, the anti-traditional Szecesszió of the rising middle class, and a "Hungarian Style" for those self-conscious about a national style.

The richness of the Hungarian urban environment in the early 20th century was not exclusive to Budapest. Many provincial cities, including the major cities of Transylvania that would be lost to Romania at the 1920 Trianon Treaty had strong concurrent urban developments with quality and creativity that rivaled the capital. Against this rich patrimony, the post-World War II urban architecture of Hungarian cities was almost as dismal as the mass-produced housing was monotonous. National policy was primarily investment in economic production. Thus the urban fabric of all the cities suffered both from lack of new capital, and the non-maintenance of their heritage. It was only in the renovation and restoration of select national historic structures and districts, such as Castle Hill in Budapest that quality in the built environment first reappeared. But generally new buildings for commerce or culture seldom went beyond the functionalist box.

A limited opportunity for new expression emerged in new multi-departmental stores. Beyond the warehouse with a sign, or the open-sided modernist box as a store, several new larger department stores made statements of place. The 1969 Imre Makovecz design for the Bodrog Department Store in the center of Sárospatak was finally completed in 1973. The adventurous exterior has an equally exploratory interior design by

Bodrog Department Store at Sárospatak, 1969–1977, by Imre Makovecz. The soft-edged building has no structural expression, contrary to most modernist designs. The flat branching forms on the side hint at plant forms.

Furniture Shops at Szentendre, 1975–1977, by Imre Makovecz. The street facade articulates wall and roof while exploring the modulation of each.

Gábor Mezei. The Makovecz search for creative form involved "a simple plant analogy, a chalice-shaped flower formation". The resulting architectural exaggeration within a single large scale concept has an expressionist appearance, especially because of the bulging and swelling forms. Within the generally symmetrical and frontal composition, the circulation and interior are developed asymmetrically. The open ground floor contrasts with the almost weightless closed shell of the floating upper story. The boldness of such a design based on a dominant total form and its unusual aesthetic resolution caused great difficulty. Designed while in the employ of the state-owned architectural practice Szövterv, Makovecz was subjected to extreme pressure from his superiors, got it built, and ultimately lost this job.

More mature was the expressive commercial corner infill in the well-preserved town of Szentendre, less than an hour north of Budapest, designed by Makovecz in 1975 and completed in 1977. It contained shops, a furniture show room and workshops, with office on the second floor. Again interiors were designed and executed by Gábor Mezei. The design fits comfortably into its resort town whose historic fabric is carefully preserved. Szentendre had its origin in the 18th century as a new town for Slovenian refugees. Today it is a thriving, picturesque artistic colony supported by tourists. Even though scarcely 20 years old, the Makovecz shops seem almost older than some of their centuries-old neighbors.

The corner site is a block from the town center. The white rendered masonry walls and red-tile roofs easily fit the streetscape. A major plan generator was a mature horse chestnut tree near the corner that inspired a small paved yard with a garden wall maintaining the building line along the sidewalk. Walled gardens are a key local element in the definition of public and private space of Szentendre. The curving swayback of the ridge line raises the roof to provide a usable second story within the attic while conforming to the scale of adjacent buildings. Equally unnoticeable may be the one symmetrical element: at the corner, the roof cantilevers forward with bulging skylight eyes in the roof, while a large shop window centered below adds to the animal imagery.

Although modest in size and scope, this design anticipated both philosophic concerns and formal responses of the next decade. The sensitive solution did much to publicly confirm the distinctive organic approach of Makovecz. But in the controlled economy of that period there were few private clients for commercial buildings, and even cases where local authorities would allow private development. Makovecz therefore survived in his private practice by working on other building types. Thus it was a full decade before he built another commercial design.

Ágasház Market at Visegrád, 1986, by Imre Makovecz. Exposed self-braced timber frames support barn-like roofs.

Ágasház Market, Visegrád

This design, the Ágasház Market at Visegrád in 1986 was a rural road-side mixed-use venture. The timber frame skeleton supporting barn-like roofs was arranged around an outdoor patio. Using logs, milled timbers, and naturally curved members, the self-braced frame avoided expensive foundation connections. The exposed structural pattern provided a characterful architectural signature while allowing maximum flexibility for infilling walls and moving partitions as shops and restaurants changed. Commanding in location is the 1979–1982 Fészek household goods department store and office Tüzép Irodaház by István Kistelegdi. It faces the 1907 Vilmos Zsolnay Statue in the Pécs square that commemorates the famed ceramist. The store is at ground level and there are two stories of offices above plus a high tiled roof. Located at the southwestern edge of the historic core of the old city, Fészek is a large block which runs parallel to the major east-west street, Rákóczi, which developed as a country access road outside the medieval fortified walls.

Fészek Department Store at Pécs, 1978–1982, by István Kistelegdi. Circular canopies at ground level; the tiled gable roof has a decorative wing pattern.

The long volume is divided asymmetrically so that the recessed major entrance is on axis framing the end of the approach street, as one drives north on Szabadsag from the railroad station to the center of the city. The wedge shapes of colored roof tile reinforce the cross axis of the building aligning it with the 194-meter regional television tower on the crest of the 530-meter ridge of Mescek Mountain that forms a backdrop.

Perhaps because of the severity of its architecture geometry the 1979 design of Fészek is not always included in lists of organic architecture. The principle elements are the circular shop windows with their pure arc hoods and the poorly detailed curtain wall between flat white pilasters. The design is cleanly distinguished and the massing is sensible: a tripartite composition with the tiled roof as "head", the glass curtain wall as "body", and the ground floor round windows as "legs". Only on the roof is there a colorful remnant of organic liveliness; the wing pattern of a giant bird in the tilework.

For István Kistelegdi, the only original member of the Pécs Group still living and practicing there, Fészek was his first major design since the 1978 dissolution of the Young Studio and the formation of a new studio by Pécseterv. Kistelegdi had gone back to the Technical University in Budapest to take courses in the Preservation of the Architectural Heritage in preparation for the scheduled urban rehabilitation of the center of Pécs. A major assignment for István Kistelegdi in the 1980s was the renovation of the Elephant Block in Pécs. Named after a well-known bar and restaurant established in the 18th century, this city block of six attached historic buildings facing Széchenyi Square, the main urban space, was comprehensively renovated between 1975 and 1988. Included in the facilities are an expansion of the Elephant Bar and Restaurant to accommodate a coffee shop and a casino. Bookstores, an ice cream parlor, and other shops are at ground level. Upstairs are offices and a library. Although every aspect of this thorough process required continuous architectural responsibility it is only in the details of furnishings and the new uses and in the courtyard landscaping where original design is visible. The refreshing built-in seats, steps, and wall that articulate the change of level reveal fluid organic sensibility.

Conservative, orderly, and traditional is the new design by Kistelegdi of the Iparos Ház or Craftsmen's Block also on Rákóczi, completed in 1988. Because of a potential widening of this major street it sits behind a wedge of public space. Here the traditional rhythm of the shop windows at the sidewalk is reinforced by projecting arches that carry the shop signage. The dormer windows for attic meeting rooms have distinctive collars that are joined together to make a continuous crenelated profile that reveals a certain playful Hungarian taste. This commercial block of rental spaces for artisans also has a quiet gar-

Elephant Block, Pécs

Elephant Block at Pécs, 1975–1988, by István Kistelegdi. View from city square, before trees and street furniture were placed.

Elephant Block at Pécs. Aerial view of historic buildings in the urban core renovated as a single integrated commercial block.

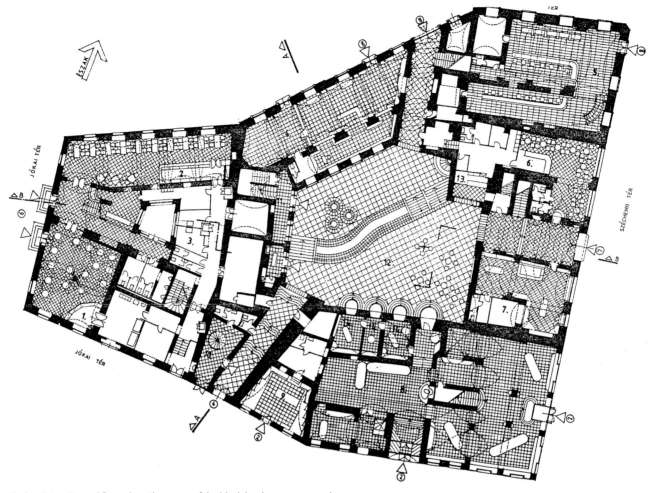

Elephant Block at Pécs. Ground floor plan. The center of the block has become a paved courtyard with outdoor cafes.

136

Craftman's Block at Pécs. Architectural elements are creative versions of historic models and spaced with similar rhythms to maintain the texture of the city. Green columns, red roof, and white walls repeat the colors of the Hungarian flag.

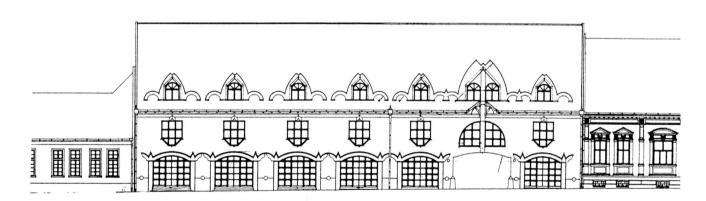

Craftman's Block at Pécs, 1985–1988, by István Kistelegdi. Drawings show how the spacing of similar elements is varied to change scale. The street elevation below has a wider spacing of windows compared to the courtyard elevation above.

Craftman's Block at Pécs. Courtyard with green-tiled colonnade provides a quiet retreat.

Roman Yard, Pécs

den courtyard with a change of grade, trees, and a raised porch with green tiled columns. The lower side has an extra story as well as a small restaurant and dining patio facing south. Located close to the urban core of Pécs this block has a certain domestic quality appropriate for its site between commercial and residential areas.

The urban renewal of the historic core of Pécs as characterized by the Elephant Block and by selective infill was a major political commitment during the 1980s that was paralleled to varying degrees of investment in a number of other provincial cities such as Szombathely, Kaposvár, and Szeged, as well as smaller centers such as Keszthely. These involved a complete overhaul, renewing services including putting electricity underground, rationalization of the public bus system, and exclusion of automobiles. Large pedestrian precincts were developed with new signage, complete street furniture, and other urban amenities. This reinforcement of each old city core was to some degree at the sacrifice of further services for the mass-produced high-rise housing blocks on the periphery of these cities. This gentrification happened in a country which had long eliminated its gentry and was almost without a middle class. The intensification in use of the urban core was economically inspired, not socially motivated.

The restoration of older buildings and outdoor spaces was by renewal and adoptive modernization, but was usually not archival preservation. The design of public spaces avoided memories or sentimentality. Unlike in Ljubljana for instance, the charismatic capital of the adjacent new country of Slovenia where episodic memorials commemorate historic events on almost every corner, the rich past of Pécs was not brought out of hiding. Although memory was critical to the agenda of organic architects and had always informed their building design it came late to urban development.

But the past reasserted itself as it were when excavation for foundations uncovered historic ruins such as at Római Udvar, the Roman Yard complex designed by Sándor Dévényi. This infill project in the middle of the block near the main square of Pécs emerges on parts of three streets, including 11–13 Teréz and 11 Jókai. Each narrow street entrance has its own architectural invention that invites exploration. Designed in 1987 it was constructed in 1990–1992 and contains shops, banks, boutiques, restaurants, and small offices. In completing the foundations, the extent of ruins of several Roman atrium houses required changing some of the structure and interior spaces. Originally the basement was to contain 40 parking places, but the number was reduced to 33 to leave the walls of the 4th and 5th centuries A.D. from the original city of Sopianae exposed and incorporated in the revised design. Thus the Roman Yard is a true meeting of cul-

Roman Yard at Pécs, 1987–1992, by Sándor Dévényi. Projecting through the pavement is a wall fragment dating back to the Romans; the rounded windows and cylindrical columns are playful references to the Roman past. The glazing at the corners and the continuous eave help to visually reduce the scale.

Roman Yard at Pécs. A weaving together of architectural elements around a pivotal column suggests the rich heritage of the city.

tures over 2,000 years. In the exuberant courtyards Dévényi was inspired by the only remaining Roman details in Pécs in the design of ten windows with consoles and engaged columns. Playful Pompeian colors are also used inside the building and facing the open courtyards. Elsewhere facing the public streets the facades are developed with less historical reference by encouraging free decorative architectural fantasies enriched by ceramist Sándor Dobány, whose work present reinterpretations of the colorful Pécs tradition of Zsolnay ceramics.

Thus, the rejuvenation of the core of Pécs has evolved in the parallel creativities of István Kistelegdi and Sándor Dévényi whose distinct talents continue the heterogeneous urban richness of Hungary with diverse organic infusions. In other communities restoration of the historic urban fabric or the village structure was less thorough, and nowhere was it easy.

Roman Yard at Pécs. The narrow entrance deliberately raises the roof of the passage and breaks the cornice line.

At Szerencs, a small town dominated by an historically important church and a sugar beet factory, the construction of the Népház, or People's Center, is characteristic.

The idea of a new mixed-use building within the town was generated around 1985 by several local organizations such as a union, the Red Cross, a restaurant owner, and the National Front who were encouraged by the leadership of the mayor and town council. Several sites were considered. Makovecz was invited by the mayor to participate. The local bank became involved when a site they wanted to expand was chosen. The public needs were modified when meeting rooms were added, room sizes were changed, guest quarters were inserted together with the concept of a covered court. First sketched in 1987 by Ferenc Salamin in the Axis studio of Makona there were many modifications during construction. In the wake of Hungary's political changes between 1988 and 1990, the client became a private company before the building was completed in 1990.

The glazed corner entrance to the People's Center addresses a major intersection in the center of Szerencs and opens into a large bright balconied hall, an architectural centerpiece, with a swelling skylight. Its glazed garden wall focuses on a church steeple on the crest of the hill behind. This civic hall is used for exhibitions, weddings, and public receptions. Elegant brass balustrades repeat the graceful curves of the branching laminated wood supports of the roof.

The major interior spaces were designed in detail since the users participated in the process from the beginning. On the one side of the hall are offices as well as the lottery shop. On the other side of the hall is a restaurant with a variety of meeting rooms behind as well as civic guest quarters. The design for the restaurant followed guidelines of a German beer company which included the use of low lamps, exposed dark timberwork, thick wood tables without tablecloths, and in general the use of natural materials, relating to the natural process of brewing.

The attached two-story bank has a separate entrance along the side. The bank was a renovation and expansion. A new mezzanine and a new higher roof was built by extending the old walls upward to support its own continuous curved skylight along the ridge.

Although the People's Center could be called a community center, it is primarily a mixed-use commercial building with some community functions. And although a relatively large building, the planar elements of the wall design stepping along the street provide an appropriately modest scale. The smooth and sweeping organic continuities are found inside: in the almost seamless delicate timber roof construction revealed above the two major interior spaces with their shapely skylights. In spite of the clarity and the elegance of the wood roof framing, it was not achieved without hidden dowels and glue.

People's Center at Szerencs, 1987–1990, by Ferenc Salamin of Axis. The community facility defines an important corner in a small town; the transparent main hall at the intersection is a local landmark.

People's Center at Szerencs. Unlike the timber struts in the main hall, the black struts in the tavern have no structural purpose.

People's Center at Szerencs. The roof structure is also expressed upstairs in the new mezzanine of the bank hall.

Most difficult to summarize – yet seminal in its impact – is the mending and reconstruction of the city center of Kecskemét over a period of 20 years by architect József Kerényi and many others. Perhaps by its nature urban design is more of an organic process than architecture which can sometimes produce results totally foreign to physical or social context. But Kecskemét had received not just benign neglect but lethal acts that had totally ruptured its historic integrity. In designing the first pedestrian street in Hungary in the 1970s Kerényi placed a concrete fountain so cars physically could not go through.

Because the town had never been rich, there was the belief that "there are no genuine monuments". But Kecskemét did have an architectural imprint. Around the center was a collection of characteristic religious buildings facing on the main square that was unprecedented in Hungary. Catholic, Re-

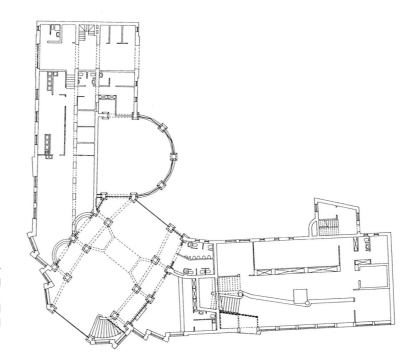

People's Center at Szerencs. Ground floor plan of old buildings with new annex. The old bank building forms the wing to the right. The newly constructed main hall is oriented diagonally toward garden at the rear and old church steeple on the nearby hilltop.

People's Center at Szerencs. Street elevation, showing stepped walls to provide a transition of scale between the major elements. Both the bank on the right and the main hall at the corner are marked with ridge skylights.

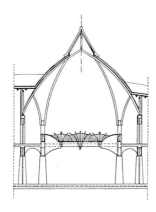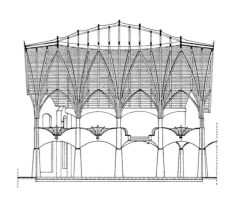

People's Center at Szerencs. Sections through the main hall show curved timber roof struts springing from white concrete columns and framing the skylight.

People's Center at Szerencs. Main hall.

formed, Evangelical, Jewish, and Serbian congregations all had a distinct architectural presence in the city silhouette together with the City Hall designed by Ödön Lechner. The main square was not a single regular square but a dynamic connected public space once occupied by the amorphous "dawn market". The buildings around it displayed a heterogeneity of styles, from Gothic to modern to "turn-of-the-century" architecture. Yet saving old houses could not yet be justified on aesthetic or historic grounds. The economic argument however allowed the conversion of the former Synagogue into a science and meeting center, and the old Franciscan monastery became the Kodály Institute of Music.

The urban rescue of Kecskemét cannot be illustrated. This welding together of many tattered fragments is the skilled result of intimate understanding and collective activity. Kerényi wore many hats from architect to member of Parliament, planner to politician. He has said, "Looking back on our recent past we understand that the memory and culture of a settlement must be preserved. Although in the human organism, the cells die and are born again during one's life, we cannot speak about a new man. The new system of cells preserves the knowledge and memory of the old one. Towns and settlements too are rebuilt and changed, but we have to continue their genetic memory". An example at small village scale is the little local restaurant and wine museum by György Koczor at Hajós. The architect volunteered his services while working in the collective practice of Delterv at Szeged. It was a commercial opportunity for the village in renovation and reuse of existing buildings instead of conversion into holiday cabins. Hajós is a low-population rural crossroads in the sandy southern plain famous for its wine. Its picturesque lanes of half-buried wine cellars were already a regional attraction and the sampling of local white wines with a lunch of country foods is a popular tourist activity.

Because the new construction uses traditional materials, the architect's contribution is almost invisible. A new curved gable end provides identity to the Hajós Cellar without signs. The Dutch profile of the gable reflects the centuries-old cultural connection of Hungarian Calvinists with Holland. The conversion is a soft urban design that merges into the natural rural order of wine cellars and sandy lanes.

The new commercial opportunities opening to every community confirmed by the political changes of 1990 were also an invitation to lose the sense of local identity and uniqueness so long cherished in Hungary. Makovecz is quite verbal about the cultural threats of the new commercialism. When one has worked conscientiously with a spirituality that unites a people for thousands of years of history, how do you respond to the sudden infusion of Western capital and ideas? New capital has come first to service industries, hotels, restaurants, and showrooms to sell capital goods. But capital dictates its own terms, just as the previous two generations of communist occupation had its own kind of cultural dictatorship. "The greater his master, the haughtier the slave." Makovecz says, "the slaves of the bankers are haughtier than the slaves of dictators". Dévényi is concerned that Hungary should not become "the backyard of Europe".

One creative organic example is the new 6,770 square meter regional shopping center "Fema" at the edge of Pécs. Fema was designed in a limited competition by István Kistelegdi in 1988 as part of a speculative investment developer team from West Germany. It was deliberately located on the main road south from Pécs to Yugoslavia before her political and economic problems had erupted. Shoppers from Yugoslavia had been expected to provide more than half the business. Fortunately, the site was also adjacent to the areas of large-scale prefabricated housing of South Pécs that had never had ade-

Restaurant, Hajós

Restaurant at Hajós, 1984–1986, by György Koczor. The newly interpreted Dutch gable on a wine bar and museum renovation recalls historical ties between Calvinists of Holland and Hungary.

Shopping Center, Pécs

Fema Regional Shopping Center at Pécs, 1988–1991, by István Kistelegdi. A lineal layout is diagonally placed on the site for easy access.

Fema Regional Shopping Center at Pécs. The narrow circulation with steps was inspired by the medieval streets of Pécs. The space is skylit and built of green stained timbers.

quate shopping facilities. Thus immediate success has been from the neighborhood.

Kistelegdi conceived Fema differently from the conventional shopping center, and he was surprised it was built. From the sky, from outer space, it is intended to be a marker, its wings on the diagonal creating a distinct landmark. On the ground he saw it as a simulation informed by medieval Pécs, which is a terraced town on the slope of a mountain, with narrow passages and steps. Every major space in Pécs has a cupola. So should the new shopping center. Since it also offered a cultural program, the center meant a frame for living, meeting and talking. Until Fema, South Pécs had only been a place for sleeping. But there were compromises. The main passage originally six meters wide was built at four meters. And while under construction the mezzanine floors were expanded and escalators added, even though the concept of the building was based on stairs. All of the anonymous case work was imported from West Germany when it could have been much cheaper and more characterful had it been built locally.

The long skylit spine of Fema is a stepped lineal enclosed street lined with small shops. The interior of rich green stained boarding is associated with the south-facing mountainside gardens of Pécs. Next to the glass cupola is a crossing of the pedestrian access with another set of main entrances from the parking lot. The servicing of the shops exposed to the parking lot is screened by curved metal trellises that are intended to be vine-covered. Probably least memorable is the department store where merchandise and artificial lighting dominate. Behind the store the main service entry is absorbed within the high building mass that addresses the major intersection.

Fema as a shopping center is more than a distinct architectural profile with questionably tight shopper circulation, although both may contribute to its vitality. It is an unexpected design, rather than the usual formula. Copper is the most expensive roofing in Hungary; you cannot easily find the entrance doors; and the oak doors stick. Yet fundamentally this architecture of sweeping curves, glazed ridges, and a forest-colored interior arcade works. Perhaps especially because it is not a perfect selling machine, it is a more attractive and memorable shopping place.

Within the core of Pécs, commercial development continued in competition with such suburban facilities. On a relatively small, deep site on Mankácsy Street just one block southeast of the city hall, Sandor Dénényi completed in 1992 a mixed and compact development, schematically simple around an open courtyard with parking underneath. The innovative architectural detailing uses classically based details with exaggerated proportions. Deep reveals play across the totally designed surfaces. Regular spacings seem to shift a half bay on each story so that columns and pilasters hang in mid air over arches. Yet everything is re-solved visually, proportions are generous, structure is sound, ma-terials are substantial, and three-dimensional integrity prevails. The materials are predominantly stone and stucco, not the boards, shingles, and timbers of earlier organic work. Yet a double roof allows timber struts and a shingled rustic canopy to crown this characterful commercial development.

Shopping center and mixed-use development, as well as new methods of financing have also influenced the design of the work environment. An exceptional experience was the design and construction of a speculative office building at 17 Paragrári in Szombathely in 1991–1992 which is now the headquarters of AB Aegon General Insurance Company. The design by Tamás Nagy of the Axis office required unusual skill and coor-dination. Four young local speculators invested both their sav-ings and took out a loan. But they demanded high-quality de-sign and construction. Because they also insisted on speedy construction it meant almost double the cost. Fortunately, con-struction took only nine months and an appropriate buyer was found. Since the site was 250 km west of Budapest the weekly architects' site visits established the rhythm of the construction.

This three-story office building near a hospital was built up to the building line in the middle of a block of old one–story houses. Thus it anticipates increased density and rising land values as it adds a distinct presence to the street. Simultaneously, a large rear yard was planned for car parking, some of it covered. An arched passage through the end of the building gives access. By placing the ground floor on a slab at grade a basement was avoided. Simultaneously, dormer windows in the attic al-lowed a full third floor of offices within the height limitations. Half of the main floor is a kind of banking space with cashiers for financial transactions. The other spaces have typical office uses. Most pleasant is the third floor where the sloping ceiling of the roof is relieved by large projecting dormers that have their triangular walls glazed and splayed open to distribute nat-ural light.

Along the street the symmetrical organization of the facade sug-gests a kind of rustic classicism. Deliberately, more permanent materials were used. Sharp hard brick give a distinct color and texture. Engaged brick columns and soft corners model the swelling walls. Console brackets at the second story support angled wood struts that carry the deep overhang of the red tiled roof. The full height of the stair hall has a central glazed window feature which is capped by a high glazed lantern that also brings in natural light from above.

Mankácsy Street Office Building at Pécs. Facing the narrow courtyard, structural columns that appear to hold up the vaults of the roof, suddenly hang in mid-air in the center of arched openings. Thus apparent structural discontinuities reduce visual weight.

Mankácsy Street Office Building at Pécs, 1990–1992, by Sándor Dévényi. The street facade displays sudden shifts of surface material, a double roof unex-pectedly extends into the street.

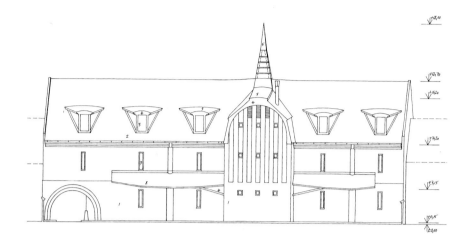

AB-Aegon Insurance Company Headquarters at Szombathly, 1990–1992, by Tamás Nagy of Axis. Rear elevation. The arch allows access to the yard space, a cantilevered canopy protects parked cars. The tower capped by a steeple contains toilets and stairs. Glazed roof dormers provide light for the attic while maintaining a low building profile.

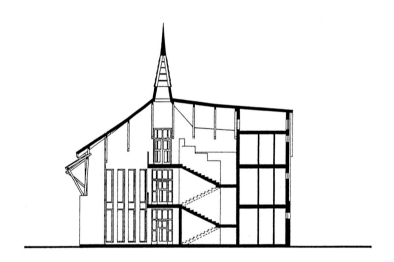

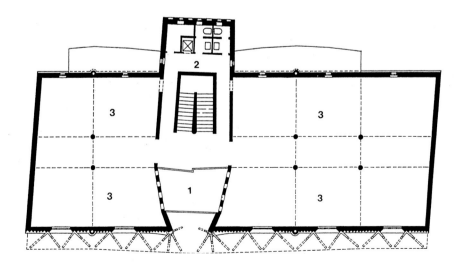

AB-Aegon Insurance Company Headquarters at Szombathely. Plan and section. Wide column-spacing allows large uninterrupted bay sizes, maximizing the useable space within the building envelope. The lobby is open to daylight from the lantern of the steeple three stories above.

AB-Aegon Insurance Company Headquarters at Szombathely. Brick details
and textures modulate the wall along
the street. Branching struts carry
a deep overhang.

Wooden Grave Posts, Kopjafa, in cemetery at Ócsa, south of Budapest. The carved head boards get shorter as the base rots, and they are pushed further into the ground.

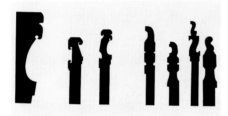

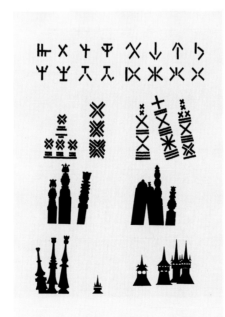

"Only From Pure Sources", Plates 4,5: "Ancient callings – messages, signs, wood cut grooves, wodden grave markers, wooden steeples."

a bow. It can also be a tulip, symbol both of Hungary and a universal sign of the fecundity of woman.

The best-known traditional grave marker is the wooden carved grave post, fejfa, or "head board". In each Protestant area and especially in Transylvania the term "kopjafa" is widely used referring to a wooden grave post or "fa kopja", traditionally the halberd or pike belonging to a fallen soldier which was stuck into the ground to mark his grave. Alternatively the term "gombosfa", or wooden knob, is used. This custom of the 16th century when Hungarian soldiers were fighting the Turks was continued as a wooden grave sign during the reformation by Protestants and Jews to distinguish their graves from the Roman Catholics who used a wooden cross as a marker. Today each village continues to have its own characteristic wooden markers that are carved by local craftsmen maintaining the shapes and meanings of the individual community.

In practice, these wooden grave posts themselves go through an organic disintegration. As the portion in the ground rots, the post is driven further into the earth. The gradually shortening post generally disappears after two or three generations just as the memory of that soul is forgotten.

During World War II the custom of marking a dead soldier was reinterpreted using a bayonet with a helmet on top. After the war these folk customs were typically replaced by machine-made work of more permanent materials such as artificial stone or imitation marble using more universal imagery. Simultaneous with the Soviet occupation came public memorials in permanent materials erected in every town and village, paid for by local subscription to honor the fallen Soviet dead. But no monuments were encouraged to record lost Hungarian soldiers. With the withdrawal of the Russians in 1991 their permanent memorials were dismembered.

In the later 19th and early 20th centuries the kopjafa traditions were discovered as authentic motifs by both scholars and designers including Károly Kós (1883–1977), in their search for a specific Hungarian style. Kós used kopjafa carvings decoratively on the porch posts of his own 1910 home, Crow Castle near Sztana in Transylvania. Again in the 1973 manifesto and exhibition, "Only From Pure Sources" these archaic shapes are primal sources. In this graphic juxtaposition of cultural memory and prememory the kopjafa together with bell towers, "harangláb", and wood carving patterns are critical relics: "Ancient Callings: … Do they still have anything to say to us, when we are searching for a new harmony for ourselves?" (Plate 5) Already among the first works of the Young Studio of Pécs was a small parish Calvinist or Reform Church by István Kistelegdi at Szamoskér in 1970 in the very eastern end of Hungary. It sits in a field as part of the tiny linear village of old houses; a sacred object without a conscious civic space. The approach

Reform Church at Szamoskér, 1970, István Kistelegdi of Pécs Group. Reform Church at Szamoskér. The church in this tiny linear village is located amidst farm fields.

walk is split by the bell tower to separate the genders; each has an entrance at opposite ends of the single-spaced hall. The massive walls of traditional sun-dried brick or adobe are structurally stabilized by the double curvature of their Baroque-like plan. The heavy roof with its wood-boarded ceiling floats over a continuous glazed strip that follows the curved top of the thick walls; this clerestory brings light in from above. Sturdy boarded pews with scrolled ends add to the substance of the interior.

The freestanding bell tower with its concrete base provides a sculptural counterpoint. It was inspired by the timber-framed steeple and four pinnacles of the traditional bell tower from the nearby village of Nemesborzova that István Kistelegdi drew up one summer as a student. Once thought to be built in 1860 it

Reform Church, Szamoskér

has now been dated to the 17th century. The original has been moved and rebuilt at the outdoor folk museum at Szentendre where it has become among the best-known images of Hungarian folk architecture. The bold originality of the Szamoskér Reform Church is the pride of this conservative Hungarian denomination. Although István Kistelegdi is usually credited alone, Zoltán Bachman and Gyula Csaba were critical to the team.

Reform Church at Szamoskér. Where the heavy curves of the symmetrical walls and swooping roof pinch together are the entrances – one for each gender.

Reform Church at Szamoskér. With aisles beside the walls, the heavy timbered pews span the space.

Reform Church at Szamoskér. The scroll profiles of the pews are derived from patterns of traditional furniture and embroidery.

Bell Tower from Nemesborzova, 17th century. Drawing by István Kistelegdi. A model for the bell tower of the reform church at Szamoskér.

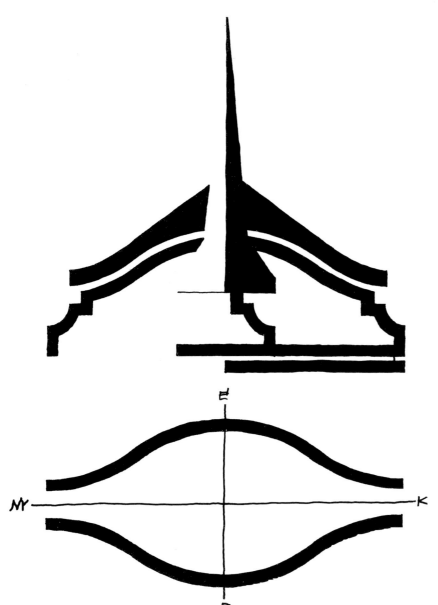

Reform Church at Szamoskér. Design sketch. Two walls under a heavy roof curve open to form the worship space. The spiked bell tower stands in juxtaposition.

Cemetery Chapel, Siklós

This village church was followed by a cemetery chapel at Siklós south of Pécs completed in 1972. Again István Kistelegdi from the Young Studio was chosen as designer since he had already done other projects for the local council. The chapel sits on a low brow beside the lane that enters the cemetery. Although an elementary circular plan with simple construction, the design is sliced by an outdoor space that serves both as a gateway to the cemetery, and as an overflow for services. The masons for the low stone walls needed to be taken to the local castle to see how stone should be assembled; such was the level of construction experience at that time. The exposed timber frame of the roof becomes a pattern of interior centralized

Cemetery Chapel at Siklós, 1972, by István Kistelegdi of Pécs Group. Beside the path into the cemetery, the circle of the chapel roof breaks open to invite entry.

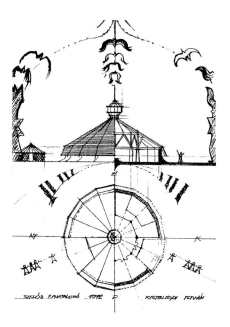

Cemetery Chapel at Siklós. Sketch study of plan and section, showing similarity to a yurt.

symmetry. The red tile roof, like a great peasant skirt, recalls the tent and the yurt associated with Hungary's Asiatic origins. The horizontal axis of North, South, East, and West are symmetrical about the central vertical axis. A crystal cupola almost free above the roof brings light into a similar ceiling crystal fixture. The circular plan and the roof framing are similar to Péter Oltai's later clubhouse in the Park at Pécs, described previously.

The Roman Catholic Church of Szent Erzsébet had been designed in 1976 and was completed in 1982 to the design of György Csete, with structure by Jenö Dulánszky. It was built on the industrial island of Csepel in the green village of Halásztelek, located near the southern suburbs of Budapest. Once a rural agricultural village, the new inhabitants were primarily workers in the Lenin Steel Works nearby. Much of the great refinement and precision in construction detail was done by pattern makers from the foundry who were parishioners.

Cemetery Chapel at Siklós. The timber framing of
the chapel roof is centered by a suspended
faceted globe that diffuses daylight from a similar
lantern above the roof.

"Only From Pure Sources", Plate 27: The Universe
in a Yurt. This instinctive human formula tailored
from orderly wood construction is similar to the
carving on grave markers; the glass lantern is like
geometrical crystal formations.

Szent Erzsébet Church, Halásztelek

The foundation of St. Elizabeth has sixteen regular sides. The building functions are organized vertically: under the ground is the crypt and above, at ground level is a floor of community meeting spaces. The sanctuary on top has a dome made of laminated timber structural segments. The faceted patterns of the oculus as well as the interlocking structural arcs exposed in the sanctuary remind one of Gothic tracery and at the same time resemble the sign and trajectory of the sun. The entrance to the sanctuary is oriented exactly along the direction of the winter equinox thus symbolizing the victory of light over darkness.

St. Elizabeth sits with obvious simplicity and clarity in the midst of a loose non-descript cluster of houses on a flat plain. The deliberate hemisphere profile is emphasized by the site design. The building is surrounded by a three-meters-high earth berm covered with sod and with red roses, the flower of St. Elizabeth. Stairs up the berm lead to a wooden bridge, a gangway

Szent Erzsébet at Halásztelek, 1976–1982, by György Csete. The church rises behind an earth dyke.

across a dry moat to the double doors into the church. The doors are almost invisible when closed since they continue the materials and shape of the exterior skin. When pivoted open they lead directly and immediately into the sanctuary.

The interior of the sanctuary is a single pure hemisphere. Chairs and pews are not fixed to the floor. The altar furnishings repeat the architectural theme. The host is a finely crafted wood globe that is a miniature of the ribbed dome. The banners designed by Ildiko Csete are printed with sun patterns, repeating the radiant circular structural forms of the plan. The only light enters through a large crystalline oculus at the zenith. The top opening connects the natural light of the heavens through the vertical axis of the sphere to the central altar.

In the origins of its concentric form the church of St. Elizabeth can be associated with elementary geometrics and with platonic solids, and thus with fundamental human experience. The

Szent Erzsébet at Halásztelek. The perfect hemisphere of the interior with its structural arcs of laminated timber is illuminated only by a faceted oculus.

Szent Erzsébet at Halásztelek. The entrance is across a wooden bridge through pivoted doors cut into the spherical exterior.

cranial form of the skull – seat of knowledge and understanding –, the dome of the sky, a helmet, and the architectural form of power all come to mind. The simple hemisphere is claimed to recall the 1000-year-old crown of Stephen I, Hungary's first great leader, who on becoming Christianized, opened the country to western Europe. Thus, the oxidized copper dome in a green village is rooted in old symbols. The architecture ties together the yurt, the Asiatic tent, assumed a part of Hungarian prehistoric origins, with the geodesic geometry of Buckminster Fuller's synergistic domes and late 20th century technology, as anticipated by plate 27 from the 1973 "Only from True Sources" manifesto.

Another episode of religious faith expressed by local determination is the circular chapel of "Our Lady of Hungarians" completed in 1984 at Cegléd. Located at No. 87 Széchéni Street, this modest complex faces the cemetery across the street. In 1978 the parish serving the northeast part of town around Fegyver Square again applied to build a chapel to replace their converted 1838 adobe peasant house, which they had used for a community of almost 5,000 since 1936. Receiving the permission to build alone took four years! But this was not the first attempt. The much-loved parish priest Gyula Zsédely admitted:

"We suffered for exactly 40 years for this new chapel. The priest who started it died in banishment and the chapel's walls were ruined. His martyrdom encouraged us to continue his work. We asked József Kerényi, architect and university lecturer, to make new plans and based on these we managed to build this jewelry box in Cégled."

The architect József Kerényi remembers:

"It was almost impossible in this small-village region to dream about a church: to build the House of God among the houses of poor people. Taking the local culture and tradition into consideration, I designed not a building, but a special composition which symbolizes the course of life on Earth. The point is: we come to the world from global space and we return to it. From the street, the global space, our way goes through the covered but open and 'gray' space to the closed and central spaces of the church. The symbol of Virgin Mary is the wreath, therefore the central space of the church is a wreath designed in a space. There is a circular, wall-bordered space connected to it. The center of it is indicated by a simple, carpentered, wooden crucifix. From this space finally we can exit to the unbordered global space, to the visual endpoint: a Calvary, formed by three trees. "The church was built of bricks, wood, stone, and concrete with a lot of sacrifice and love."

The architect, József Kérenyi, assisted by Gyula Letanóczky, provided not a single building but a miniature cosmos. Enclosed within four high walls that bound the property is a separate bell tower within the larger enclosure of a cloister with 49

Chapel, Cegléd

Our Lady of Hungarians at Cegléd, 1981–1991, by József Kerényi. Rear facade.

Our Lady of Hungarians at Cegléd. From the street, the bell tower is seen behind a roofed entry arcade, as the priest moves from the sacristy to an evening mass.

arches that lead to the tiny chapel. A mature oak tree and a separate building as a sacristy are also parts of the complex. A pelican fountain symbolizing the nurturing of the young was completed in 1991. But most intense is the spatial tension between these elements, a complexity bounded by light, space, and growing things. Newly planted trees continue the idea of the sacred grove.

The crescent plan of the chapel walls focus natural light on the altar and the white marble Madonna by Miklós Melocco. A central stone column branches at the top into timber struts that support the glazed lantern that is part of the folded geometry of the wood-covered ceiling. Hung between is a floating balcony with organ and choir that add to the intimacy. Beyond the altar window a partially enclosed circular courtyard open to the sky provides a spatial transition.

Although the traditions of Bulgarian and Moldavian village churches inspired both the forms and the enclosure, this design

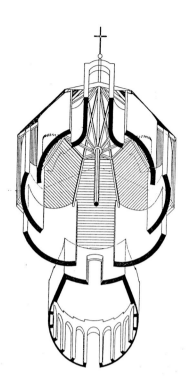

Our Lady of Hungarians at Cegléd. Spatial projection of chapel and enclosed garden space above the plan.

is no historical imitation but a fresh vision of old patterns and new worship forms. The Hungarian colors of white walls, red tile roofs, and green trees add clarity. The delicacy of the chapel and the modest scale of the entire complex is appropriate to a poor parish in a small town in the north central part of the Great Plain. But every entry through the gated cloister is a celebration in personal scale and individual experience.

In 1987 the design was nationally honored by the Ministry of Housing. In 1992 the Interfaith Forum on Religion, Art, and Architecture, centered in the USA, gave an International Architectural Design Honor award to the church and its architect, traveling to this tiny parish in Cegléd to bestow and celebrate the honors.

Even more modest and more traditional is the bell tower designed by Zoltán Rácz in front of József Borsos' famed 1930 Mortuary at Debrecen. Completed in 1991, four poles are trimmed at their top ends with the boat ends reminiscent of ancient grave posts in the eastern part of Hungary. A small shingled roof protects the bell which tolls at the conclusion of each funeral service.

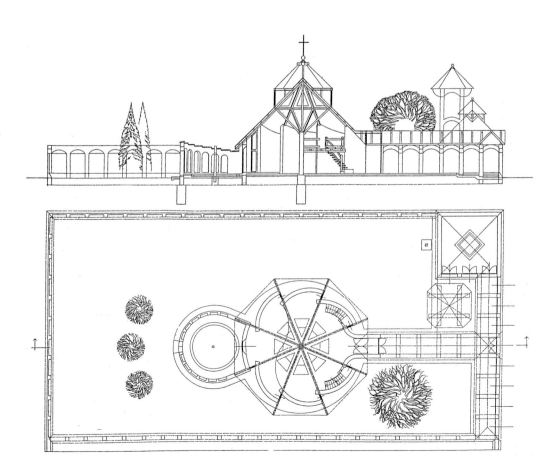

Our Lady of Hungarians at Cegléd. Site plan and section shows the enclosing wall, and the circular chapel with its attached garden wall. The bell tower stands near the street and near the square sacristy.

Cemetery Bell Tower at Debrecen, 1991, by Zoltán Rácz. Like oversized wooden grave posts, four carved poles support the protected mourning bell.

Farkasrét Mortuary Chapel, Budapest

Farkasrét Mortuary Chapel at Budapest, 1975–1977, by Imre Makovecz. Closed chapel doors clad with wood profiles resembling great feathered wings anticipate the layering technique of interior.

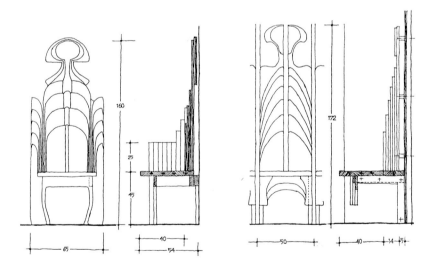

Farkasrét Mortuary Chapel at Budapest. Furniture design and construction by Gábor Mezei. Drawings for the anthropomorphic chairs show how growth, motion, and depth are suggested by the successive contours of layered planes of wood.

An even stronger individual experience is the powerful 1975 Mortuary Chapel design of Imre Makovecz for the Farkasrét cemetery in the Buda hills suburb of Budapest. Remodeling an existing space from the 1930s, it is the central of five identical side-by-side rectangular bays that open like garages to a paved plaza. The arrangement of the bier and its flowers is accomplished behind two great closed doors, detailed with overlapping boards like feathers on huge wings. When they are swung open at the time of the service, the sunlight, birds, foliage, and people, i.e. the living daily world from the plaza look across the threshold toward human remains transfigured in death, held in a dark wood ribbed cave. In his diary Makovecz wrote that the space should resemble the chest of a man, his ribs of hardwood and the dead should lie on the place of his heart. Others have seen a "whale belly" that "interprets the biblical myth of Jonah, a prophesy of Christ's Resurrection and of the resurrection of the dead through trust in God".

The dynamic shape of this symmetrical cave belly is heightened by the undulating "backbone" down the center of the ceiling and the highlights of successive rib profiles. The organic anthropomorphic rhythm of this layered rib cage is reinforced by built-in stalls against the walls that allow mourners to hover in the shadows supported by the high wings of fixed seats. These stalls for mourners exude intense human presence even when unoccupied.

The detail and execution of this moving wooden interior was completed in 1977 with the collaboration of furniture designer and craftsman Gábor Mezei: "I would like the furniture I design to be 'memorable', to be accessible to the memory, and to mirror a certain moral attitude ... Today, we hear a great deal about the issues of economy, mass production, mass demand, design. These things do not interest me. I admit that is why the only thing for me is to design objects which, first and foremost, stand for 'human dignity.'"

The only major example of organic architecture in the 2-million-inhabitants capital of Hungary, this cemetery chapel is not universally popular, especially with grief-loaded mourners. At first the official press attacked the design for reviving romantic and backward rural ideas beyond its "exceptional consonance with the vigil of grief". Others such as sociologist István Magyari-Beck in describing contemporary Hungary as "the Culture of Frustration" identify "a necrophilic dimension" to this architecture as an indication of how "Central Europe is only half European". That emotive power which Makovecz calls "building being", or "building creatures", épület-lény, multiplies the drama of an already emotive event.

This first masterwork for the architect was also pivotal in his career. Makovecz left his position in a large bureaucratic state of-

Farkasrét Mortuary Chapel at Budapest.
Exterior detail of wing-like doors.

Farkasrét Mortuary Chapel at Budapest.
The interior space is synthesized by
the successive and changing profiles of
wood cutouts.

fice to join one of Hungary's forestry companies, Pilis, as its lone architect. Simultaneously the materiality and symbolism of his architectural language moved completely to wood, to the trees and timber that were also the most accessible materials in Hungary, physically and spiritually.

A decade and a half later that transformation of milled dead wood into living architecture broke forth in the interior of the Roman Catholic parish church at Paks completed in 1990 by Makovecz. Hovering at the tip of interior tree columns and breaking through the ribs of the wood vaulting is a heart-shaped skylight invisible from the outside. Timber members now move through space independently, each a vector of energy describing and connecting figures in space. The plan form of mirror-imaged scrolls repeats the popular symbolic notation of a traditional Hungarian honey cake, or lovers cookie, and recalls Hungarian embroidery as well as Celtic runes. The sign of the double S curve repeats throughout the long site that is only two houses wide and located in an older and nondescript part of the community.

Immediately down the hill from the infamous Paks concrete panel block apartment houses of 1976, the church's sweeping elongated towers center old village houses. A silver moon and a golden sun crest the lower pinnacles. The cross on the tallest provides a distant and supreme landmark. Fine-scaled dark slate tiles are sensuously draped over subtle curves providing ambivalent dimensions that swell upward in the swollen energy of unfolding growth. Occasionally the continuity shifts. The slates do not fit the double curvatures tightly and set up slight perturbances as if ruffled by the wind. Swelling grass-covered earth berms extend the bulbous roof forms. They separate and isolate the interior into a more mystic space accessible only through the centralized processional between the two towers. The Paks church is a small, almost tiny building, seating 100. But its great exterior presence transcends its modest size. Unlike the single powerful monolithic idea of the Farkasrét interior, Paks has many overlapping interior ideas. The bilateral symmetry and the use of wood are continued with the mature skilled collaboration of the same interior architect and craftsman, Gábor Mezei. This dynamic interior is developed as an aedicular landscape. Two identical pavilions, topped with a wooden dome, flank the altar, as sheltered subspaces within the forest bower. They bring small celebrations such as baptism within the central embrace. The clergical ceremony seems incidental to this architectural liturgy of timber and light.

The powerful dominance of the towered bilateral front facing south is reinforced by two elongated gilded wood sculptures by László Péterfy. Flanking the sides are the archangels of St. Michael and St. Gabriel with raised arms and wings, and metal-tipped wooden feathers. Their harmonious overlapping

Catholic Church, Paks

Roman Catholic Parish Church at Paks, 1987–1990, by Imre Makovecz. Dark slates from Spain cover the amorphous swelling roofs. Crowning the pinnacles, the gold sun on the left, and silver moon on the right, are surmounted by the cross in the center.

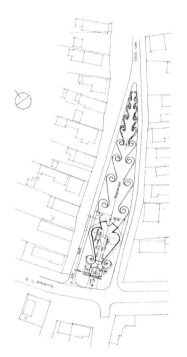

Roman Catholic Parish Church at Paks. The site plan repeats the floor plan pattern of the church.

of three layers of feathers suggest the multiple images of other architectural details also softened and stained by rain, such as the scale-like slate tiles.

These deliberate tactile statements are no preparation for the rear of the church where the wrapped closures of the tiled roof are tucked into a cleavage under the heart, and then unexpectedly break open in flared cantilevered skirts that shelter a sanctuary-like outdoor space. In contrast to the double enclosure of the interior, this is an invitation for a drive-by ceremony or a lingering event in the linear sacred park anchored by the formidable dark church presence at the far end.

In every generation one or two works of architecture simultaneously epitomize a culture for a moment and transcend the age. Paks is one of the most sensitive and contemplative spiritual spaces of this time. The serenity of its primal and mystic interior has little need for iconic explanation or reference. Vertical ribs flying free of the swooping overhead deck rush toward the light of the sky in the smell and glow of unfinished wood.

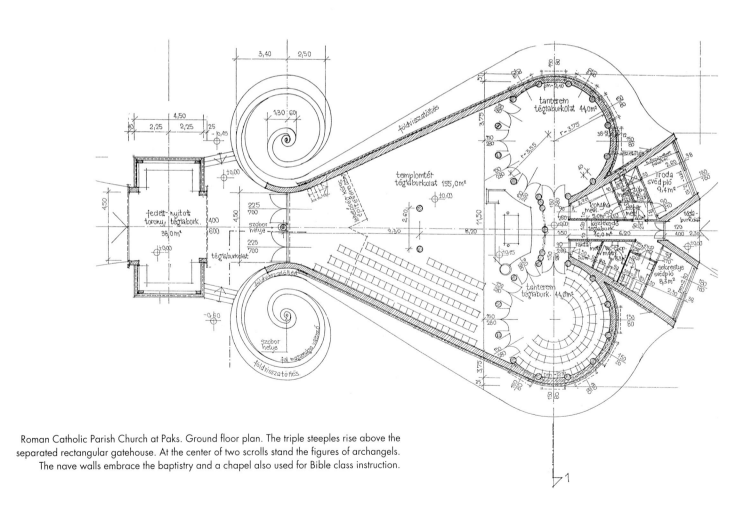

Roman Catholic Parish Church at Paks. Ground floor plan. The triple steeples rise above the separated rectangular gatehouse. At the center of two scrolls stand the figures of archangels. The nave walls embrace the baptistry and a chapel also used for Bible class instruction.

Roman Catholic Parish Church at Paks. Inside the church peeled tree trunks, milled timbers, laminated bents, and finely sawn sticks visually fuse, modulated by sunlight. Figures carved by László Péterfy.

Roman Catholic Parish Church at Paks. Timbers as vectors of the spiritual energy of trees reach upward and disappear in the shadows.

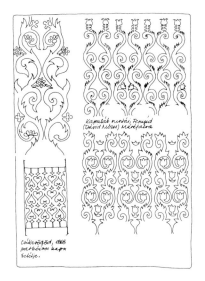

Roman Catholic Parish Church at Paks. Sketch book studies by Imre Makovecz. Folk patterns of carved boards in gates: On the left at Csíkrögöd, 1868, and at Fenyéd, Máréfalva, both in Transylvania.

Roman Catholic Parish Church at Paks.
Gilded wood figure of archangel by
László Péterfy.

Roman Catholic Parish Church at Paks.
View from the meditative rose garden to the
north of the church.

Roman Catholic Parish Church at Paks. At
the back, the distended swollen roof forms
under the heart-shaped skylight burst open
with a flair that provides a canopy for an
outdoor chapel.

On a more modest scale is the Reform or Lutheran Church in Siófok by Imre Makovecz initiated in 1986 and dedicated in June 1990. The building celebrates the 75-year determination and conviction of its priest Martin Joszef. Located in a fenced wooden grove a few blocks away from the noisy summer resort boardwalk along the south shore of Lake Balaton, its animistic appearance is enhanced by the garden of trees. Grass-covered berms eliminate exterior walls. Its realization with the contributions of congregations from Germany and Finland is a reflection of European support in Hungary but also due to the German and Scandinavian tourists in Siófok during the summer. Such help from outside countries has only been permitted since 1986. Even so the construction was not easy.

Makovecz believes a building does not just start to function when it is completed and taken over for regular activities but begins its life with its conception. Thus, for the architect, constructing a church enhances the mysterious art of building itself.

Lutheran Church at Siófok, 1986–1990, by Imre Makovecz. The face on the entrance tower animates a red-tiled horned roof. Walls are invisible behind grassed earth berms.

beam at a uniform wall height. These arched beams carry the exposed roof structure of thin wood members that form a high singular nave. The wooden roof is larger than the walls and floats above them, joined by concealed horizontal glass. Natural light from outside is reflected under the overhangs so that the entire underside of the floating roof construction is mysteriously flooded with light from bottom to top, especially early or late in the day when the sun is low in the sky. Knotty timber pews with high-profiled ends have their silhouettes repeated by the curved edge of a wooden wainscoting below white walls. Thus although the exterior walls have a uniform simple plan, the layering of materials and light add to the lateral dimensions and to the serenity and grace of the space.

At the altar, the columns are more closely spaced and point upwards toward infinity. On top, framed against the apex of the roof is the carved wooden figure of Christ ascending from the grave. Perhaps such an image is unusual in a Protestant church but it is the singular piece of figurative art within a very architectural light machine of wood. As a whole, this mannered flight of religious fantasy hints at a certain dark quality that suggests the earliest Hungarian myths and beliefs. The Siófok Church thus explores the animistic and biomorphic themes of Hungarian culture.

Lutheran Church at Siófok. Daylight reflected up underneath the skirts of the overhanging roof floods the interior with light when the sun is low.

Lutheran Church at Siófok. The wood feathers symbolize eternal life unfolding.

Creative Resistance

Culture and Change

The appearance of organic architecture in Hungary could be regarded as an aberration; caused or allowed to happen by circumstances that no longer apply. Now that a more liberal and representative political system is in place, organic architecture may not have a role. It can no longer be seen as an inventive, professional response to foreign domination and to repressive political conditions, as creative resistance. But now there may be other types of potential foreign dominance. New spiritual needs and new material conditions raise questions about the continuity of a movement assumed to be based on folk culture. Self-renewal is fundamental in any healthy organism and essential for survival. Thus, sustainability is an issue for the organic moment itself as a professional discipline. But now in the 1990s, biological sustainability begins to guide global material responsibility for the built environment in which each region and social entity must have a decisive ecological role. Hungarian organic architecture also grew out of an educational and professional system. The Technical University of Budapest with the only professional program in architecture in Hungary had a critical and unwitting role in the many events of this period. The present university was known earlier at the Royal Hungarian Polytechnical Institute and was the successor of the Joseph Technical School founded in 1844. Although education for architects and engineers in Hungary started in 1763, the Collegium Oeconomicum did not survive long. The formal beginning of a distinct program in architecture was in the appointment in 1870 and 1872 of the two professors who would dominate a half century of professional education. The program was based on the Prussian system of architectural education with its strong emphasis on technical subjects sometimes at the expense of historical, aesthetic or cultural content. Participation by Technical University students in the community was well demonstrated on the sunny morning of Tuesday 23 October 1956 when the people of Budapest found their city posted during the night with handbills: The Sixteen Demands of the students of the Technical University became the trigger that launched the bloody ill-fated 1956 Hungarian Uprising.

A unified curriculum had already been split in 1948 into architecture to educate designers, and civil engineering to train construction specialists. In 1950 three independent departments were added and registration jumped from 817 in 1950, to 2,545 in 1953. By the late 1950s the Russian impact of political as well as architectural post-Social Realism forced a retrenchment into a more unified program. It was during this period that the first generation of organic architects was educated. The 1960s were years of non-stop reform, revision and temporary curricula. Already between 1947 and 1949 all practicing architects were assembled into large state-owned and directed offices, described as "the best at the bottom and the worst at the top."

For architects, centralization came very quickly with finally perhaps 20 huge offices, many with 600 or 800 professionals. Typically, the leaders of these collective offices were not primarily professionals but chosen because of their political reliability. The orientation was like in a military organization toward the power structure and not to the work.

Also at Technical University, beginning in the late 1940s, academic positions were given exclusively to professors following the party line. Many other faculty members were released. Directions came from abroad, especially what and how to produce. The need to know the rules and the techniques was emphasized, not artistic ability. There was little interest in personal involvement. The socialist commitment to equal rights to work operated against knowledge and experience. Thus a professor of architectural history who was a former insurance agent was known for his fear of having anyone around who would challenge his limited knowledge.

These same attitudes about the uniform right to work also affected the construction industry. Skilled craftsmen were dying out. Nor were fine building materials available. When the young organic architects began to construct their first designs it was a practical imperative that they be built out of the most ordinary materials and be tolerant of the most ordinary construction craft. The gradual elaboration of architectural form and the gradual refinement of construction craftsmanship have been the patient results of deliberate nurturing by many including the organic movement.

Thus familiar and earthy building materials, such as adobe and timber were the only choice to begin organic architecture in Hungary. They were not used for sentimental or ecological reasons. By definition they belonged to the locality and by their use they became materials of affection and of a natural economy. From the beginning this goal of organic architecture as an integral extension of nature was deeply intertwined with local resources. The Pécs Group had proclaimed in 1973:

"The Region: We can create the natural unity of the region in our building through the principle of organic deduction. The building follows the forms and silhouettes of the region gradually stepping down to the zones of man. As the sculptural contours of buildings increase they approach natural forms, uniting with them, the region absorbs them.

"The formula for the solution equals again the gradual evolution away from, and then the return to natural forms." (Plate 6, see p. 24)

Thus the disruptive hiatus of international modernism was seen as a crude and temporary condition of the built environment. Beyond the figurative harmony of forms in nature is the implication of sustainability in the ecological role of architecture. In his poetic description of shelter in the exhibition catalogue Hajlék, György Csete wrote:

"The form of the bending bough is like all the ancient building forms. The roundness of mass formations contains the budding force, their silhouettes resemble trees, haystacks and hills. Solar houses should be organized according to the order of the tree of life. Thus the living spaces are connected by an attached greenhouse that economically and ornamentally tempers the heating and cooling. This is the first step toward the environmental mutuality of later eco houses, of solar collectors and wind generators especially in areas when electricity is not available. Greenhouses should be part of living architecture, not the polluting energy of today but pure solar energy in design."

But these directions were never practiced. Solar architecture and the discipline of bioclimatic design were not part of organic architecture as it evolved. It would be tempting to include the Experimental Passive Solar House 1982–1986 at Pécs by János Szász, or the skillful passive houses in Budapest and Szentendre by Gellert Kuba as seeds. But these internationally important examples and a number of other solar and energy-conscious initiatives were developed from a different spiritual as well as material base. The incentive to save energy in Hungary had not been great. As in other parts of Central and Eastern Europe, the ready availability of cheap natural gas from Russia together with the provision of inexpensive housing in a socialist state distorted the free market economics operative elsewhere. Low-cost district heating and advantageous local resources also contributed. For instance in the village of Jászkísér all larger buildings including the village hall are heated by geothermal water at 89° C. But for Makovecz, fossil fuels are not irreplaceable resources, but the animate remains of ancient creatures, our ancestors.

Choices of construction materials and assemblies also reveal issues of resource renewability and sustainability. With the 1992 Rio conference on Global Environment and Development, architects worldwide began to examine their practices. For instance should one build with renewable resources such as wood, or with permanent materials such as stone, or recyclable materials such as steel and aluminum? When Makovecz was asked why he used wood as the major structural material for his buildings he stated that the Hungarian steel industry at the end of the 1970s was in bad condition. A decade later it was ready to collapse. At the same time the Hungarian timber industry was well-developed and the workers had a strong personal intelligence and ability. And timber framing was still very effective in spanning large spaces. Makovecz himself demonstrated the artistic possibilities. So the compromise was to use chemical fire retardents on wood and avoid imported steel.

But there were other incentives in the architectural use of wood. During the counter reformation the western part of Hungary returned to the Roman Catholic fold while eastern Hungary became a Lutheran and Calvinist stronghold. Since Hungary was then part of the Habsburg Empire, religious tolerance had been a particular issue. The law was enforced that the Protestants could not build churches of permanent materials. Hence the origin of the wooden church tradition.

More recently with the 1920 loss of over 60 percent of its territories in the Trianon Treaty following World War I, there was a law in Hungary against building with wood because there was almost no forest left. That law only changed with reforestation after World War II. But although systematic forestation was practiced in all parts of the country, the supply did not meet the demand. By 1990 wood was becoming expensive again, and Hungary began to import from its neighbors on all sides, from Russia, Czechoslovakia, and Austria.

In the evolution of Hungarian organic architecture many individuals contributed, participated, and extended ideals in varying ways, in differing intensities, and at particular moments. Fundamentally it was a collective work that resulted in a body of hundreds of buildings. All were designed by graduates from the architecture program of Technical University. But one could identify at least three major leaders of the organic movement who emerged independently in parallel. Born two years apart, each was a very different personality, from a very different background. Each in finding his own way formed a small and dedicated working group. They worked separately, developing and expanding their circle and their respective influence and effectiveness. Only then did they discover the others, met and recognized each other.

József Kerényi (born 1939) had reconstituted the city of Kecskemét in the twenty-year period between 1964 and 1984 through the state planning office of Bácsterv. He then moved back to Budapest as part of the Hungarian Institute of Town and Regional Planning. In 1988 he joined the faculty of the Technical University. In 1984 Kerényi received international recognition as an Honorable Mention from the UIA, the Union International d'Architectes, the Prize for the Improvement in the Quality of Human Settlements. The award, in memory of Sir Robert Matthew, past President of the UIA, was made for "his outstanding work in restoring and developing the town of Kecskemét." Yet also his diverse and modest-sized architectural designs have received increasing attention.

György Csete (born 1937), who seeded the Pécs Group continues to be a convincing teacher, and a part-time instructor at the Technical University without the recognition of a full academic position. Yet there he has been a design instructor of most of the organic architects in Hungary. He has also been an honorary professor in Pécs at the Mihály Pollack Technical College and a visiting professor at the University of Innsbruck since 1986. There he has offered annual outdoor workshops for architecture students in the structuring of space. He continues to enter competitions, to design buildings on commission, to act as an ethical conscience of the profession and to produce films. Although all of these are collaborative activities, he fundamentally works alone without a constant team.

Imre Makovecz (born 1935), the self-propelled and defiant fighter, has continuously accelerated in the number of design ideas and in professional recognition both nationally and internationally. His three-person-partnership Makona of 1984 had developed by 1991 into five associated design studios with 40 on staff. Even though each studio was autonomous, and there were no shared or centralized facilities, each of the 40 people had direct access to Makovecz. Internationally recognized as the most visible and vocal champion of Hungarian Organic Architecture, he expands as a great leader in conceptual thinking and design ideas. His fearless energy and creative production continue to challenge the "loss of presence" endemic to communism that now escorts capitalism.

By the late 1980s as the general ideas of organic architecture became more pervasive, these three leaders met less frequently. By 1990 each had assumed new and divergent roles. But all three were included in an exhibition on Hungarian Organic Architecture held at the Venice Biennale in September 1991, along with 34 other colleagues. The exhibition catalogue sponsored by the state Ministry of Culture and Education provided the summary document of this stage of the organic movement. Yet the notion of three leaders is too arbitrary both in its number and its suggestion of equal contributions. At some moments there were eight contributors who were vital, at others, only one or two. At a minimum, one more talent might be added to the trilogy: Sándor Dévényi belongs more to Pécs than any of the imported Pécs Group. Born in Pécs and brought up in a house by the well-known pioneer modernist Molnár, he was early sensitized to the role of architecture. But born in 1948 he belongs to a younger and transitional generation. His high-fashion design and brilliant personal decorative skill perhaps require a more generous definition of place, of "Hungarianness", and of the organic movement.

Within the organic movement, the new generation were typically rushed into professional practice. Everyone had started almost from ground zero since there was no cadre of older professionals with a well-developed expertise in this new way of

thinking including construction techniques. Thus the young had to invent almost everything from planning concepts to materials and details. This necessity together with a belief in personal authorship of the unique and original somewhat repeated the freshness and the enthusiasm of the early days of other new movements such as the Bauhaus. But by 1991 organic practice had matured.

The most important new organization of organic architects was the Károly Kós Association, Kós Károly Egyesülés. It was a cooperative of practicing offices dispersed around the country with goals of intellectual stimulation, apprentice program, and professional support. All offices had combined architectural and engineering services and most also managed construction work. The intent was to build the country up again starting at the bottom with independent small offices that have the reinforcement of a structured network of like-minded offices. Such a scheme extended the experiment of organic architecture into an experimental practice. The Károly Kós Association started in 1987 with six offices, but had ten by 1990. Each office contributed a half million forents or $ 50,000 U.S. to a common fund in addition to other participation.

The apprentice program known as the Traveling School was a curriculum with coordinated professional experiences for recent architectural graduates. Selected candidates were employed for six-month periods, rotated among offices of the member organizations for a maximum of three years. Thus they became familiar with the various conceptual and practical working methods of master architects from different parts of the country. The school offered lectures and other events focused on the program.

The Károly Kós Association also organized cooperative quarterly self-improvement retreats scheduled during the solstices and equinoxes with lectures and seminars as well as business meetings. Held at changing locations these meetings provided exposure to different settings together with new ideas. In addition each member office was committed to providing professional programs in their local community as a contribution to public education. In 1990, the Association began to publish a quarterly journal. Its name "Országépiíö", Country Builder, has multiple meanings, dealing not only with organic design and construction within the country, but also in nation building.

Collectively the Károly Kós Association represented a large networked pool of talent and experience for larger projects. With the opening up of the country to foreign investors, the scale and complexity of new development had multiplied. The group provided a strong professional basis for joint ventures.

The emergence of corporate identity of the Károly Kós Association represented one aspect of the transformation of the organic movement toward professional sustainability. But while Imre Makovecz was central to the concept and energy of this new formation, neither György Csete nor József Kerényi belonged. They could not afford to participate financially, nor could they necessarily benefit since both were independent designers without support teams. They were often involved in projects primarily as consultants. However, Tibor Jankovecs and István Kistelegdi, old associates of the Pécs Group were critical members. Thus the former model of the parallel working groups of different leaders had been transformed into this new corporate entity of many networked offices, some with several studios involved in many interactions.

This newly unified front of Hungarian organic architecture now addressed the explosive development of a surprisingly pristine countryside. With the exception of Budapest, the villages, towns, and cities had begun to be mended. Yet many parts of Hungary continued to be quite unspoiled by the commerce of the late twentieth century found elsewhere.

Early in October 1989 without mass rallies or barricades in the streets, the Party renounced Marxism and renamed itself the Hungarian Socialist Party. Within the month the People's Republic of Hungary adopted a new constitution for the Republic of Hungary. The preamble states, "All power belongs to the people". In the free elections of the spring of 1990 the Socialist Party finished fourth, only to rebound into power in 1994.

In parallel with the rapid political changes people began buying and selling everything in the rapidly unrestricted marketplace. Hungarian architects also faced new and vast choices from the construction materials and methods developed in Western Europe and the USA together with enormous amounts of technical information about manufactured products for building. Makovecz called it an "information fog", a kind of knowledge pollution that adds layers of "facts" between an object and its true meaning. He regarded this as poisonous as some of the chemical issues of outgassing and physical degradation of the built environment caused by new materials technology. His response was to hold them at arms length. In effect he would prefer the traditional materials of the region over newly created building products. Traditional houses are chemically much safer and thermally more comfortable than new apartments. Thus he exercised global responsibility in acting locally by using both local traditions and unconscious knowledge, with deliberate concern with both objective and esoteric spheres. Such organic practice was by definition multi-folded.

For some of the organic architects of Hungary the freedom of the 1990s with its western capital brought a hard and complex new dictatorship. Perhaps western investors did not need this kind of expensive architecture, which is labor-intensive, highly crafted, slow to build, over-structured, and perhaps odd in appearance. In 1982, at the opening of the cultural center in Sárospatak, Makovecz commented on the architect's responsibility:

"We trust architecture is able to salvage us from such a time-abyss, such an age of the artificially created amnesia, that tried to make people forget their ancient mysteries, origin and targets by a Golem-like informational and technological system. And we are to impede it."

Makovecz further explained that partly because he was born in Hungary and partly as he learned from Rudolf Steiner, that to be Hungarian is not just to be another person in an identifiable country. Rather there is a people spirit, a single and very large living entity, that has a quite separate identity from nationality or ethnicity. How could a western business venture be interested in that? The organic movement was also threatened by its own success. The international recognition that resulted from representing the country at the 1991 Venice Biennale could make it appear to be a national style. But in the Preface to the Venice catalogue, György Fekete, Deputy State Secretary of the Ministry of Culture and Education identified that it was creative spirit, and not the common forms that distinguished this group:

"They are joined by the conviction that man is an integral part of nature. ... A conscientious architect must not undertake to spoil his organic environment. ... Consequently, we have to give up the selfish aggressive creativity that always wants to rewrite geographical maps. These participating Hungarian architects are characterized by their endeavor to create a particular quality: their desire for a persistent presence in everyday life, their double efforts of creation in a minority situation, and the realization of individual's demands without creating 'mass-produced' works."

This dedication was reinforced by Makovecz in his Foreword to the Biennale catalog:

"As Central Europeans annexed to the East, there is nothing to be gained by our telling the big world all we have learned in this strange, hermetic, experimental world where we have had to live in the past seventy or eighty years. Neither is there anything to be gained by asking if the West needs our knowledge.

"Working according to our own laws, ideas and necessities, has been of great value to us in spite of our broken self-confi-

dence and the condition of our improvised motherland. We hope especially that the ever increasingly introspective West will realize at last what we have been dealing with, perhaps even acknowledge this strange region, called nowadays the Third World, which we built up and where we live. ...

"But it would be a mistake to think that this mission is only a stylistic inquiry. I do not believe in that concept of "style" as it has been used recently in architecture and other realms. Much more, I believe in dramatic collaboration of architects, clients, and users. I believe in ancient dramaturgic rules, and in Fate. I believe that these buildings are dead ciphers of God, where we are able to follow the voice of a withdrawing God, and find our only relief before Death. We want to erect buildings that make us remember our origin and ancestry. ..."

Yet the increasing international popularity of Hungarian organic architecture also puzzled many native Hungarians especially from the capital, Budapest, who continued to regard this substantial body of works as a folkish quirk. They forget how the Hungarian experience is full of the eccentric, the odd and inspired, and the subconsciously informed.

The pivotal building of 1990–1992 both within Hungary and abroad was a design that clearly marked the end of an era and the beginning of a new. The Hungarian Pavilion at EXPO 92 Seville by Imre Makovecz was also among the most popular of the 95 pavilions during that world's fair, and confirmed international recognition.

Makovecz was intrigued by the location of the Hungarian pavilion, just to east of the Austrian pavilion, a parallel to their geographic relationship. And the Hungarian pavilion was to the west of the Vatican pavilion across a large road. He was also inspired by the Hungarian history of St. Stephen and the Christianizing of his kingdom around 1000 A.D., and the conflicts with the East in the succeeding centuries, including the 150-years Turkish occupation at a time when Spain and western Europe were exploring the New Worlds to the west. But these critical generators were absorbed and sublimated in the design and were not obvious in the experience at Seville.

The complex design was based on the interactions of several simple ideas. Seven spiky magic steeples asymmetrically pierced a smooth rounded artificial hill covered with black tiles. This roof was like an overturned boat. Only by referring to the plan could one understand the integrity of its eccentricity. The diameter of an oak tree, the single object on display determined the placement of the sixth steeple. Then the line of towers was set at a slight diagonal toward the entrance. The intersections between this axis and the ribbed roof enclosure established both the formal tensions and the interior spaces.

This was not a building to shelter an exhibit, but a work of building art that was itself a total exhibition object. It was architecture of participation, not observation, simultaneously melancholic and vivacious. Hungary could have been presented easier with a sweetened folksy building and some peasants dancing. But here the ambiguities were more shrill. An asymmetrical but ordered composition it was quiet and remote along the ground with blank walls of grass and hanging dark slate. This continuous swollen surface of bulbous pregnancy was pierced by pinnacles with gold and silver tops. The sun and the moon shone below the cross, which celebrated the sixth tower and turned to realign the plan axis.

Against the sky the pavilion was richly inventive and eclectic. Half-familiar steeple profiles broke into new forms of bird wings and corner Gothic openings with hooded beaks. There were promises in this architectural message of multiple patrimony. The five steeples aligned on their own angled axis spiked the hidden halls between earth and sky. The sixth steeple crowned by the cross turned its orientation. The seventh steeple, shorter and more substantial with its owlish facade like Siófok marked the exit.

The visitors, in groups of about 70–80 people, followed a precisely prescribed path. Five separate "sound and light" scores played remotely to them in each distinct space. It was an environmental play using architectural sequences as sets. All was within a vast dimly lit ribbed shed, where the ridge line between the two timber shells symbolized Hungary as a meeting between East and West.

The six-meter-high, wing-like pair of timber gates swung open silently to a wedge-shaped hall with a floor ramped upwards to closed doors. Then the gates closed again automatically. The visitors group was sealed inside a windowless wooden vessel. The sconce lights on the ribbed enclosure brightened, then dimmed, timed with the music from hidden speakers. Human sounds, snatches of speech and song, percussion and acoustic memories were coupled with images and light.

Hungarian Pavilion at EXPO 92, Seville

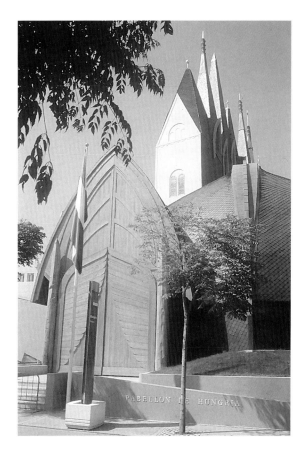

Pavilion of Hungary at Expo 92 Seville, Spain, 1990–1992, by Imre Makovecz. Exterior. The great entry doors.

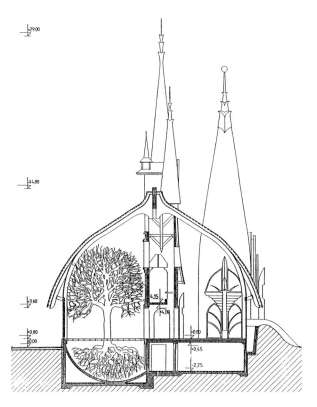

The crowded corridor climbed into six connected small rooms located midway up within the structural cages of the towers. Natural light filtered down through the matrix of their solid wood timbers. The density of angled heavy frames was reminiscent of the experiences inside the bell towers of Transylvania, such as Mezőcsávás. Through the glimpses of daylight and the outdoor sounds of those high belfry openings one again had a remote connection with the outside world. High in the towers were specially cast bells hanging, beautiful, taut and mounted ready to again celebrate the 1456 European victory over the East, of Hungary over the Ottoman Empire.

Then the forward doors opened and one descended by curved stairs into the long Hall of the West circling around the dead oak tree cut at its base by a glass floor. It was lean and bleached. Its sparse crown, barkless and leafless, was shorn of twigs. Then the top of the tree went dark and the white chamber under the glass floor was illuminated. A tangled ball of short washed roots was revealed with a few long stray underground anchors that had searched widely for sustenance. The hidden half of the tree, the secret below ground was revealed. This naked relic of a once whole tree beside the Danube was the most photographed motif at Expo '92.

Pavilion of Hungary at Expo 92 Seville. Cross section. Crown and roots of the oak tree occupy similar spaces above and below the floor. The full basement is necessary for services, its light well lies behind an earth berm. The tallest tower rises above 29 meters.

Pavilion of Hungary at Expo 92 Seville. Sketch elevation of the seven towers emerging from a great hill.

Then the closed portals under the bell towers quietly opened to the great oblong Hall of the East. One passed through the base of the towers underneath the squeezed corridor. Here the grand architectural confrontation finally unfolded. The angled wall of vertical bell towers intersected the insistent curved ribs of the symmetrical roof of the building in a 270 square meter cavernous hall. The architectural dilemma was revealed and celebrated.

Makovecz had anticipated some of that experience in his Preface to the 1985 exhibition catalog Magyar Élö Epitészet, Living Architecture:

"Here in the Carpathian Basin where the one-time Scythian and Celtic empires existed, a certain light shines through the ground, the inner light of the native land, that midnight sun which is the Sun of the spirit driven underground. The light of this Sun changes our houses into special beings between Sky and Earth. They are parts of meta-nature which is the continuation of nature itself."

The Pavilion was truly a Hungarian building in a foreign land and an alien climate. It was a fresh composition of Makovecz's best abilities in a powerful spatial object. Historians can trace the parts. Biographers will enjoy the detective search of origins. Makovecz was no longer the organic architect who with each new design began again to reconceive the fundamental architecture of his native land. Now with this design he reconsidered the essence of his past quests. His new layers were built on the old explorations. But he had never before created a building so restless and so provocative!

Until this Pavilion, Makovecz's buildings had often been designed frontally with a strong bilateral symmetry reinforcing the closed entry plane. Once penetrated, a bold axis of mirror-imaged elements revealed a rich open interior with intricate side subspaces. But at the Pavilion the interior spaces were hermetically separated, and the path of progression was a knot: angled and curved, it actually looped back like a figure eight under its earlier position, funneling, constricting, releasing and exploding through dynamic architectonic chambers. The potential collision of trabeated towers and ribbed vaults, of two form cultures, became an architectural dialectic between distinct ordering systems. The result was not cacophony, but a spirited new concord, both dynamic and understandable, successively revealed as one progressed.

Unlike many other exhibits, the timbers of Hungary were real. The perfume of solid wood construction reinforced the environmental theater. The exposed timber framing, the trim slate shingles, and the folded copper flashing were soundly built. The lighting was thoughtful. Its programmed sequences compressed within seconds the revelations of form and enclosure that could otherwise unfold only by time and experience. The sound and

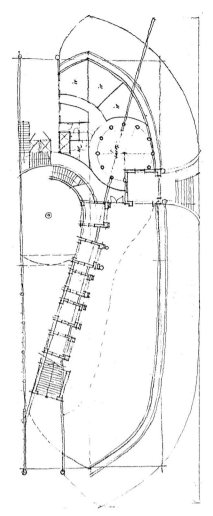

Pavilion of Hungary at Expo 92 Seville. Sketch plan, showing diagonal circulation access up the stairs and through the bases of the row of towers, whose location is determined by the oak tree. The smaller circle of columns contains the restaurant.

Pavilion of Hungary at Expo 92 Seville. In the summer twilight, gold and silver finial accents gleam above the eccentric bell towers.

film effects underlined the clarity, rhythm, and tension of the architectural intention.

At Expo'92 the two most popular objects on display were not high-technology wizardry, but natural objects: the 60-ton Antarctic iceberg of Chile, and the Hungarian dead tree. The Hungarian oak was poignant. Here the dead tree was interpreted freshly as the epitome of life. Simultaneously it was murdered and stripped at its prime. Dried and bleached it expressed the essence of life more vitally than any animated model. Mortality must mean life, since nothing can die that did not live. Inside his wooden building, Makovecz revealed this tree's life-filled soul.

Dr. Béla Kádár, Executive Commissioner of the Republic of Hungary and Minister of International Economic Relations

Pavilion of Hungary at Expo 92 Seville. The elusive black-tiled hill of the pavilion is surmounted by a mirage of bell towers.

Pavilion of Hungary at Expo 92 Seville. The oak tree of life with roots visible through the glass floor in the Hall of the West.

wrote: "I would like our exhibit to be a surprise for you! A surprise, because you did not know us in this way, and a discovery ..." The Hungarian pavilion was indeed a discovery for the world at Expo. Solidly built of ancient dreams, nostalgia, yearnings, and hints of nightmares, it was brilliantly creative and memorable in becoming anew.

In the evolution of organic architecture in Hungary each decade has characterized a particular role. The 1960s were a time of conception, insemination, and gestation; the 1970s saw the birth and young childhood; and the 1980s witnessed puberty, adolescence and the exuberance of early adulthood. This maturity was first recognized abroad. By the beginning of the 1990s it was confirmed by the Hungarian government commissions for Venice and Seville. As the 1990s continue the important infusions of a new generation of architects and of their newly identifiable studios broaden and enrich the professional culture of Hungarian Organic Architecure. Creative resistance based on these hard-won values is now challenged by new political and cultural realities within Hungary; and by the globalization of international commerce that dilutes identity and meaning everywhere.

Lorinc Csernyus, Budapest
Elementary School and Community Hall, 1987–1992, Csenger

György Csete, Budapest
Spring House at Orfü, 1970–1974, Pécs
(with Pécs Group)
Precast Panel Apartment Blocks, 1972–1976, Paks
(with Pécs Group)
Szent Erzsébet, 1976–1982, Halásztelek
Katai House, 1979–1986, Szentendre
Cattleherd Inn, 1985–1990, Balaton Szentgyörgy
(with Gábor Sánta and FORMA)

Sándor Dévényi, Pécs
Tannery Reconstruction as Museum of Pécs, 1975–1985, Pécs
Hillside Terrace Houses, 1977–1979, Pécs (with Csaba and Weiler)
The Blasted Block, 1978–1985, Pécs
Formwork on concrete wall along Aradi Vértanúk, 1979, Pécs
Wedding Hotel, 1982–1985
Bull Head Block, 1982–1989, Pécs
Aquarium Terrarium, 1983, Pécs
University Cellar Club, 1984, Pécs
Villa, 1986–1988, Mecsek Mountain at Pécs
Infill House on István, 1987, Pécs
Pensioners Apartments, 1987–1991, Paks
Roman Yard, 1987–1992, Pécs
House that Eats Flats, 1988, Málom at Pécs
Mankácsy Street Office Building, 1990–1992, Pécs

Dezsö Ekler, Budapest
Dance Barn, 1986, Téka Camp at Harangod, Nagykálló
Dining Shelter, 1987, Téka Camp at Harangod, Nagykálló
Baths, 1987, Téka Camp at Harangod, Nagykálló

Lookout Tower, 1988, Téka Camp at Harangod, Nagykálló
Reception Hall, 1989, Téka Camp at Harangod, Nagykálló

András Erdei (deceased)
Woodcarvers House and Structures, 1979–1982, Velem
Wood Storage Shed, 1979–1982, Velem

Tibor Jankovics, Keszthely
Resort Hotel, 1977, Fadd-Dombori (with Pécs Group)
Phoenix Hotel, 1984, Keszthely
Rammed earth Csaladi House, 1984–1985, Zalaszentgrót
BM Sanatorium and Therapy Pool, 1984–1991, Héviz
(with Bcáta Lukács of Forma)
Sports Club, 1986, Keszthely
Gösser Beer Garden, 1991, Keszthely (with Tibor Bárándi of Forma)

József Kerényi, Budapest
Our Lady of Hungarians, 1981–1991, Cegléd
Urban Center, no date, Kecskemét

István Kistelegdi, Pécs
Reform Church, 1970, Szamoskér (with Pécs Group)
Cemetery Chapel, 1972, Siklós (with Pécs Group)
Elephant Block, 1975–1988, Pécs
Fészek Store and Offices, 1978–1982, Pécs
Rákóczi Street Apartments, 1984, Pécs
Anna Street Apartment House, 1985, Pécs
Craftsman's Block, 1985–1988, Pécs
Weisz House, 1987, Mohács
Fema Regional Shopping Center, 1988–1991, Pécs

György Koczor, Szeged
Hajós Cellar, 1984–1986, Hajós

Zoltán Koppány, Budapest
Temporary Exhibition Pavilion, 1985, Budapest

Attila Köszeghy, Debrecen
Homok Street House, 1985, Debrecen

Apafi Street House, 1986, Debrecen

Imre Makovecz, Budapest

Restaurant Haifisch, 1963, «Cápa» at Valence
Sió Csárda Inn and Restaurant, 1964–1966,
outside Szekszárd
Szövosz Camping Structures, 1966–1967, Balaton Szepezd
Roadside Restaurant, 1968–1969, Tatabánya
Bodrog Department Store, 1969–1977, Sárospatak
Cultural Center, 1974–1982, Sárospatak
Duna Restaurant, 1975–1976, near Szentendre
(with Gábor Mezei)
Furniture Shops, 1975–1977, Szentendre
Farkasrét Mortuary Chapel, 1975–1977, Budapest (with
Gábor Mezei)
Camping Facilities: Picnic Shelters, 1976–1977, Visegrád
Village Center, 1976–1984, Zalaszentlászló
Camping Facilities: Lavatories, 1977–1979, Visegrád
Camping Facilities: Family Cabins, 1977–1979, Visegrád
Ski Lift and Ski Bar, 1980, Dobogókö
Mogyoróhegy Resort Restaurant, 1981–1983, Visegrád
Rákóczi Street Apartments, 1982, Sárospatak
Village Center, 1982–1985, Jászkisér
Nature Study and Cultural Center, 1982–1988, Visegrád
Bus Shelter, Toilets and Kiosks, 1983–1984,
József Loránt House, 1983–1984, Zalaszentlászló
Lajos Gubsci Double House, 1983–1986, Buda Hills
Pete and Megyeri Duplex, 1983–1986, Buda Hills
Village Center, 1983–1987, Jászapati
Village Hall, 1984–1986, Bagod
Community Center, 1984–1993, Szigetvár
Village Center, 1985–1988, Bak
Sports Hall, 1985–1989, Visegrád
Community Center, 1986–1996, Kakasd
Dóczy House, 1986–1988, Göd
Ágasház Market, 1986, Visegrád
Lutheran Church, 1986–1990, Siófok
Kiss House, 1987–1991, Debrecen
Roman Catholic Parish Church, 1987–1990, Paks
Tibor Jakob House, 1988–1991, Solymár
Arpad Vezer Technical High School, 1989–1993,
Sárospatak
Pavilion of Hungary at Expo 92, 1990–1992, Seville,
Spain

Ervin Nagy, Budapest

Pharmacy House Apartment, 1983–1985, Sárospatak
Meeting Hall, 1984–1986, Ceglédpuszta

Tamás Nagy, Budapest

AB-Aegon General Insurance Company Headquarters,
1990–1992, Szombathely

Péter Oltai, Budapest

Youth Club House, 1972, Balakányi Park at Pécs

Zoltán Rácz, Debrecen

Cemetery Bell Tower, 1991, Debrecen

Ferenc Salamin, Budapest

The Cave, Design/Build Camp, 1982–1983, Visegrád
People's Center, 1984–1990, Szerencs
Extension and Remodeling Secondary School,
1986–1989, Fonyód
Apartments, 1986–1989, Gyöngyös
Végvári House, 1989–1993, Miskolc

Benö Taba, Miskolc

Bükk Forest National Park Entrance, 1984, Miskolc

Gábor Urr, Budapest

The Tower, Design/Build Camp, 1985, Visegrád

László Vincze, Budapest

Apartment House, 1987–1990, Gyöngyös
Sports Hall, 1987–1992, Csenger

Architettura Organica Ungherese/Hungarian Organic Architecture/Magyar Organikus Építeszet. La Biennale di Venezia 1991 – V. Mostra Internazionale di Architettura. Kós Károly Association. Budapest, second edition 1992. Hungarian and English plus 4 page German insert. 128 pages. (The second edition contains corrected text and revised English translations.)

Baktn, Ferenc and György Máte, eds. *Liberated Hungary – 1945-1960.* 1981. Budapest.

Bodor, Ferenc, ed. *Nomad Generation, Youth and Folk Art in Hungary. 1970-1980.* 1981. Budapest.

Boersma, Tjeerd, ed. *Imre Makovecz, Hongaars Architect.* 1989. Rotterdam: Nederlands Architectuurinstituut. Exhibition catalog, 96 pages. Dutch.

Bognar, Botond. guest ed. *Architecture Plus Urbanism. A + U.* Tokyo. No. 234, March 1990. "Contemporary Hungarian Architecture." p.7–126. Japanese and English.

Cook, Jeffrey. "Imre Makovecz." *Friends of Kebyar.* Portland, Oregon. 1987. No. 35; "György Csete and the Pécs Group." 1990. No. 45.

Cook, Jeffrey. "Back to Earth", *International Architecture and Construction.* n.d. (1994). London. Vol.1, No.2. pp. 41–48.

Cook, Jeffrey. "Makovecz in Organski Nacionalizem." *Arhitektor Bitten.* Zagreb. 1988. No. 7–8. pp. 61–64.

Csete, György. *Hajlék.* A Pécs Csoport épitészeinek Kiállitása a Budapest Kiállítóteremben 1987. 32 pages, Hungarian.

Eifert-Körnig, Anna Maria. *Die kompromittierte Moderne: Staatliche Bauproduktion und oppositionelle Tendenzen in der Nachkriegsarchitektur Ungarns.* 1995. Berlin: Reimer. Published in cooperation with Uj Müvészet, Budapest.

Ekler, D. "The Architecture of Imre Makovecz." *Architecture and Society.* Sofia, Bulgaria. 1987. No.6. pp. 64–67.

Annually published, in English and Russian, summaries in French and Spanish

Ekler, Dezsö. "Seele und Form", *Archithese.* 1987. Zürich. No. 3, pp. 31–38. German

Erdei, András. in *Architecture.* 1984. Washington, D.C., September.

Erdei, András. in *A + U.* 1990. Tokyo, March, No. 234.

Ferkai, András. in *Criticism in Architecture,* 1989. Concept Media, Singapore, for the Aga Khan Award for Architecture, pp. 102–103.

Ferkai, András. in *Piranesi.* Ljubljana, Slovenia. Vol. 3, No.4. 1994. English.

Frank, János. *Makovecz Imre.* 1980. Budapest: Corvina Kiadó.

Gadney, Reg. *Cry Hungary! Uprising 1956.* 1986. New York: Atheneum. p. 16.

Gerle, János, and György Szegö. *Építésziti. Tendenciak Magyorszagon 1968–1981.* (Trends in Hungarian Architecture) 1981. Budapest. Exhibition catalog. Hungarian.

Glancey, Jonathan. *Architectural Review.* 1981. London, March.

Glancey, Jonathan. "Makovecz Embrace". *Architectural Review.* 1984. London, October, pp. 34–40.

Glancey, Jonathan. "Imre Makovecz." *World Architecture.* 1989. London. No. 2. pp. 40–55; No. 38 (1995).

Greene, Herb. in *Progressive Architecture.* 1962. New York, May

Greene, Herb. *Mind and Image.* 1976. Lexington: The University of Kentucky Press.

Halász, Zoltán, ed., *Hungary.* 1960. Budapest: Corvina. pp. 133–137.

Köszeghy, Attila, and Andrea Sasváry. *Kapuk Ablakok Ornamensek Debrecen Belvá Rosában.* 1985. Debrecen. Sponsored by the city architect, its 15 page essay is followed by almost 200 pages of photographs and drawings of historic facades and has become a pattern book used by many to copy.

Kerényi, József. in *Mágyar Épitömüvészet*. (Hungarian Architecture) 1976. Budapest. No. 4 et al.

Kerényi, József. in *Bauten der Kultur*. 1979. Berlin. No. 4.

Komjáthy, Attila. *Imre Makovecz*. 1977. Budapest: Mai Mágyar Müvészet.

Kroö, György. *A Guide to Bartók*. 1974. Budapest: Corvina.

Kunt, Ernö. *Folk Art in Hungarian Cemeteries*. 1983. Budapest: Corvina Kiadó.

Magyar–Beck, István. *Mágyar Épitömüvészet* (Hungarian Architecture). 1989. Budapest. No.4.

Mágyar Élö Épitészet/Hungarian Organic Architecture. 1985. Budapest: Beresenyi. 164 page illustrated catalog edited by members of the Visegrád Workshop.

Mágyar Épitömüvészet (Hungarian Architecture). Budapest. Four to six issues annually. In Hungarian, with captions and some articles also in English, plus summaries in four to six other languages. Beginning with an article on Makovecz in 1966, works of the organic architects have been published as part of continuous national coverage of all new architecture in Hungary. See Vol. LXXXIII, 1992, No. 4 for articles on Seville Pavilion, etc.

Makovecz, Imre. "The Form of the Roof", *Architecture and Society*. 1984. Sofia, Bulgaria. No.2, pp. 18–21.

Makovecz, Imre. "Living Architecture". 1987. A conversation with Zoltán Nagy, translated by Gabor Lorant, AIA. Unpublished.

Makovecz, Imre. "Bauen bedeutet Magie". *Archithese*. 1987. Zürich. No. 3. pp. 24–28. German.

Makovecz, Imre. in *Makovecz*. Toronto: University of Toronto. Catalog includes translation of Judit Ossko's interview with Makovecz on Hungarian Television, 1988.

Makovecz, Imre. in *Transforming Art*. 1991. Sydney, Australia. No.5. Transcript of interview with Nigel Hoffmann.

Malonyay, Dezsö. *Mágyar Nép Müvészet* (Hungarian Folk Art). Budapest: Franklin-Társulat. A series of monographs, often undated, published in 1900s, 1910s.

Moravánszky, Ákos. "Tendenzen in der ungarischen Architektur des 20. Jahrhunderts" *Bauform*. Vienna. No. 99/100. Architektur in Ungarn 1900 bis heute. pp. 11–29. German.

Moravánszky, Ákos. "National Orientation of Hungarian Architecture During XX Century." *Architecture and Society*. 1985/86. Sofia, Bulgaria. No. 4/5. pp. 200–203.

Moravánszky, Ákos. "Fire Walls: Central Europe's Intensity and Hungarian Architecture." *Daidalos*. 1991. Berlin. No. 39. pp. 50–63.

Natchev, Zdravko. "Imre Makovecz" in Emanuel, Muriel, ed. *Contemporary Architects*. 1980. London/New York: St. Martin's Press. pp. 506–507.

Nemzetközi Alkotobátor. International Workshop Seminar 1983 Budapest: Technical University. Hungarian and English.

Nemeskürty, István. *Hungary in Seville. Guide to the Hungarian Pavilion at the Seville World Exhibition*. 1992.

Országépiiö (Country Builder). Published by Kós Károly Egyesülés (The Károly Kós Association). Budapest. Quarterly, 1990–1994 64 pages, illustrated. Hungarian.

(Pécs Group.) *Only From Pure Sources*. 1973. 31 unnumbered plates, published privately in 1000 copies.

Tradition and Metaphor/A New Wave in Hungarian Architecture. Perinne Ja Vertauskuvat/Unkarilaisen arkkitehtuurin uusi aalto. 1981. Helsinki. 54 page catalog in Finnish of the exhibition organized primarily by András Erdei jointly sponsored and shown at both the Museum of Finnish Architecture and the Alvar Aalto Museum.

Tradition och Metafor/Nio Ungerska Arkitekter. 1981. Stockholm: Arkitekturmuseet. 59 page catalog in Swedish of the Helsinki exhibition reconstituted.

Zsédely, Gyula, and Jószef Kerényi. *Journal of the Interfaith Forum of Religion, Art and Architecture*. Winter 1992–1993.